THE
SURE
THING

THE SURE THING

The Making and Unmaking of Golf Phenom Michelle Wie

Eric Adelson

 BALLANTINE BOOKS · NEW YORK

Published in the United States by ESPN Books, an imprint of ESPN, Inc.,
New York, and Ballantine Books, an imprint of The Random House
Publishing Group, a division of Random House, Inc., New York.

BALLANTINE and colophon are registered trademarks of Random House, Inc.
The ESPN Books name and logo are registered trademarks of ESPN, Inc.

Library of Congress Cataloging-in-Publication Data

Adelson, Eric.
The sure thing : the making and unmaking of
golf phenom Michelle Wie / Eric Adelson.
p.   cm.
ISBN 978–0-345–51175–1 (hardcover : alk. paper)
1. Wie, Michelle. 2. Golfers—United States—Biography. 3. Women
golfers—United States—Biography. 4. Success—Psychological aspects.
I. Title.
GV964.W49A44 2009
796.352092—dc22
[B]   2009015485

Printed in the United States of America on acid-free paper

www.ballantinebooks.com
www.espnbooks.com

1 2 3 4 5 6 7 8 9

First Edition

Book design by Susan Turner

To Dad

CONTENTS

● ● ● ● ● ● ● ● ● ● ● ● ● ● ●

The Next Tiger Woods Is…
a Ten-Year-Old *Girl*?

In August 2000, I flew to Honolulu to report a story for *ESPN The Magazine* on the most popular sports figure in the Aloha State at the time, University of Hawaii head football coach June Jones. While I waited for Coach Jones in his office, the school's sports information director, Lois Manin, started telling me about a local golfer who could drive a ball 300 yards.

I confess I was only half listening. People pitch ideas to magazine writers all the time, and someone who hit big, booming drives didn't sound like a rare find in golf-crazy Hawaii.

But Manin persisted.

"She's 10 years old."

She?

Ten years old?

Manin scribbled a name on a blue Post-it note: B.J. Wie. She added a phone number. The girl's name, Manin told me, was Michelle.

I returned to my hotel in Waikiki and forgot about it. The next day, I opened my notebook and saw the Post-it. I was curious. So I called and left a message for Mr. Wie. He returned my call the following day. He had a soft, almost airy voice, and often punctuated his sentences with a laugh.

"Michelle has a very normal childhood," he said of his young daughter before I even thought to ask. He offered to put Michelle on the phone—again, before I even asked if she was home. I heard him place the receiver down on a table. Soon there was a light rustle.

"Hello?"

Her voice was high-pitched, barely audible. I introduced myself. I had not really prepared for this interview. Was I really going to write an article about an athlete who wasn't even a teenager?

"So you like golf?" (I had to start somewhere.)

"Yes!"

"Why's that?"

"It's fun!"

Fun? Fine, but I wanted to see if indeed this 10-year-old really did live a "normal" life. So I asked her what she liked besides golf.

Michelle plunged into a long explanation about the differences between Digimon and Pokémon.

"What else do you like?"

Laura Ingalls Wilder—"the writer," she explained—and Gelly Roll pens. She rattled off her favorite toys as if drawing up a list for Santa. She said she loved all kinds of animals, especially big, fluffy dogs.

"But not amphibians!"

(Noted.)

"Who's your favorite golfer?"

"Tiger Woods."

"Oh, yeah? Think you can beat him?"

"Maybe in five years."

I smiled and listened for a laugh, any sign of a joke.

Silence.

She was serious.

Two years earlier, ESPN had launched the first issue of its magazine with a cover featuring four athletes it crowned as "NEXT"—Alex Rodriguez, Kordell Stewart, Eric Lindros, and Kobe Bryant. All four would have big careers, *ESPN The Magazine* predicted, but they would also bring forth a revolution in their sports. Rodriguez was a rare gem at the time, a power-hitting middle infielder. Stewart was a double threat at quarterback who could throw and run. Lindros was a one-of-a-kind power forward: Gordie Howe with speed. And Bryant had stormed into the NBA without so much as a single college game on his résumé.

Michelle Wie, at the time I first spoke with her, had the potential to break more molds than all four of those athletes. If she could hit a golf ball 300 yards at age 10, what would that mean for the game of golf down the road? What kind of force would she be in the game when she grew up to be, say, 18?

Michelle Wie got a page to herself in *ESPN The Magazine*'s November 27, 2000, issue:

Aloha! . . . When I was 5, I hit a drive 100 yards. I had to start playing on courses after that because my drives would always go into the neighbor's yard. During the summer, I play 18 holes and then practice. I start at 9:30 a.m. and play until 8 p.m. In the winter, I wake up at 6:30, and my mom drives me to school at 7:45. I have math, science, Spanish, art, and PE. I like science the best. During recess, I play basketball with the boys. School ends at 2:45. I do my homework in the car. Then I play. My parents take me to Olomana Golf Course. I play 9 or 18 holes and then chip and putt. My mom carries my clubs. My dad watches. . . . I used to play with Travis and Chris. They're 15-year-olds. But they avoid me now because I out-drive them. I usually hit the ball 230 yards. Sometimes 250. One time I hit it 300. I won every tournament against people my age, so I've been playing older kids. I like being better than them. On the weekends I watch golf on TV . . . the PGA Tour, not the LPGA. I like the players on the PGA Tour better. I want to play on the PGA Tour.

My favorite golfer is Tiger Woods. I think I can beat him in the near future.

Like when I'm 15.

Over the next five years, Wie became a household name in Golf Nation. The youngest golfer to win the Hawaii Women's State Amateur Stroke Play Championship. The youngest to win the Jennie K. Wilson Invitational, the state's most prestigious amateur tournament for women. (When a local reporter sought her out for a quote afterward, he found her at a table, grinning, with remnants of an ice-cream sundae all over her face.) The youngest to qualify for a Ladies Professional Golf Association tournament, at 12. The youngest to win a USGA championship, at 13. The youngest to enter a PGA Tour event, at 14.

At 15, she landed on the cover of *Fortune* magazine and as a guest on *Late Night with David Letterman*. At 16, Wie was named one of *Time* magazine's "The *Time* 100, The People Who Shape Our World"—in the "Heroes and Pioneers" section no less, with the likes of former president Bill Clinton and Nobel Prize winner Elie Wiesel. Clinton and Condoleezza Rice both went out of their way to play a round of golf with her. (The secretary of state fawned over her sparkling nail polish.)

Wie handled all the fuss and bother with grace and aplomb. It was as though she expected all of this to happen. And then, as she got near the brink of realizing the prediction she made over the phone as a 10-year-old, everything changed.

THE SURE THING

"It's Not That Difficult Being Me"

The man never sat down on a golf course. Never. He stood like a sentry at all times, behind the tee or on the side of the fairway, with his binoculars in play, ready to flip open his notes on the greens, ready to let out a whoop if his daughter made a big putt.

And yet on this Friday in May 2006, Michelle Wie's father found a lush patch of grass on a steep hill overlooking the 13th green at the Sky 72 golf course just outside Seoul, and he sat down. He smiled as he took in the sight of his only daughter, Michelle, lining up a tricky left-to-right 15-foot putt for birdie. That was something rare for him, too—smiling before a big putt.

But this was a special occasion.

This was one of the happiest days of his life.

From where he sat, B.J. Wie could see the highway leading into the city where he and his wife were born. He could see cars filing away from the cloisters of skyscrapers huddled along the

Han River. He knew most of the people in those cars could pick out his daughter in a crowd. So many of them took pride in her achievement, as if she were one of their own, even though she had been born in America. So many wanted to bring up their children to be just like his daughter.

And with good reason. Michelle Wie commanded a reported $700,000 in appearance fee money to play in the SK Telecom Open, a tournament on the Asian Tour with a $600,000 purse. Then there was the $50 million in endorsements she had already locked up . . .

Money, though, was only one reason B.J. grinned. He could have lounged on that hill all day and reflected on so many other wondrous things about his daughter. Michelle was a straight-A student, a kind soul, a beautiful girl, an accomplished athlete, and one of the most famous teenagers in the world. And she was competing against men, one of her biggest dreams, in an official sanctioned professional tournament, something she had done three times before at the Sony Open in her native Hawaii.

What made this day truly special to B.J. Wie was that his daughter was a virtual lock to make the cut. And that was why, basking in the glow of those reveries about one of the most famous teenagers in the world, his daughter, B.J. looked like a man sitting on top of the world.

The moment Michelle stepped up to her ball, B.J. hopped back on his feet. He watched her move her putter back and forth, then saw her Nike One scoot toward the hole, only to lip out. Par. B.J. beamed anyway. Michelle, only 16, was at the top of her game, at 5 under par for the tournament with only five holes to play in the second round. Five holes away from becoming just the second woman since 1945 to make the cut in a men's tournament. Anything could happen; B.J. knew that. But he also knew his daughter's game, and he knew in his heart that she wouldn't falter.

As always, Michelle was being pursued by a pack of photographers. Every newspaper and magazine editor in South Korea (and the rest of Golf Nation, for that matter) wanted pictures of Michelle Wie—for her beauty, for her fashion, and most especially for her immaculate swing.

Yet for all the photos, few knew much about the young girl behind the celebrity. Most knew that she hailed from Hawaii and was the hottest new thing to hit golf since Tiger Woods. But she revealed little about herself in interviews with the media, other than the odd joke about school or a stray comment about a favorite movie. Her parents rarely spoke to the media at all, so they were no help in enlightening people about their daughter.

Most fans didn't know whether she had a boyfriend (no), a pet (no), or a sibling (no). They didn't know what her parents did for a living. (Dad was a professor of transportation engineering at the University of Hawaii; Mom was a real estate agent in Honolulu.) They didn't know that she was going to a high school in Honolulu whose graduates included Steve Case, cofounder of AOL, and Barack Obama, then a first-term U.S. senator from Illinois who would go on to bigger things.

The one thing everyone did know, the one thing no one could forget, was her golf swing.

Starting at the bottom, the swing began with feet large enough to require men's size 11½ shoes. Those feet gave her such a solid base and balance that she could stand on half-domed medicine balls in her socks, swing an iron, and hit a golf ball as straight and far as if she were standing in her spikes on the ground. Most golfers, male and female, roll on their feet as they power through the swing. If you focused on Michelle's feet as she swung, you got no hint that she was doing anything but standing still.

Her legs were long—she was already 6'1", at age 16—and her thighs strong as stone pillars, but there wasn't a trace of gawkiness or awkwardness in her gait. In a full swing, her torso twisted and turned as if on a swivel, and her shoulders rotated around her spine like a propeller. Her long arms effortlessly carried her hands to the top of her backswing, then through the ball and all the way over her left shoulder in a fluid pendulum motion. Those hands were soft and feminine, yet strong enough to whip a club around her body like a light saber. A normal adult man's grip strength—roughly 80 pounds—diminishes to 45 or even 40 at the apex of a golf swing. Wie's grip strength was 120 pounds, double that of a normal grown woman and equivalent to that of a full-time male carpenter.

The combination of Michelle's size, flexibility, and strength gave her enough torque to bend a golf club into a blur. The result: shocking power.

At her appearance on David Letterman's show the year before, when she was 15, he asked her how far she could drive the ball from the tee. Michelle answered with a shrug: "About 300, maybe 320." Letterman buckled over in laughter. The crowd burst into cheers. Wie smiled and laughed, too, but seemed a little perplexed at their response: to her, it was just something that came naturally. To everyone else, it was . . . impossible.

And though everything about her body screamed power, everything about her soft and delicate face whispered fragility. Her smile came easily (at least it did back then, when everything was going well), never coming across as forced or false. Her laugh was like a soft giggle, a near hiccup. She never seemed hurried. She hid the power as well as she hid her emotions. And yet, even at 16, she exuded femininity, almost without knowing she had it.

"Physically," said friend and LPGA veteran Christina Kim, "she's got the body of a rockin' 25-year-old. She's a hot chick."

Michelle Wie looked blissfully unaware of the pressure she faced and the history she was making. Was she simply too young to understand? She answered that every time she arrived at a tee and swung a club. Her jaw jutted, her mouth disappeared, her eyes narrowed in certainty, even coldness.

Yes, Michelle Wie knew exactly what she was doing.

So Wie heard the racket of the cameras and even noticed the cars idling on the highway so that their drivers could catch a glimpse, yet she tuned it out in the same way she had tuned out the occasional cell phone chatter, the planes flying low overhead, and even the shouts of "Hot body!" from men in the crowd. It was the same way she tuned out the skeptics, the women golfers back in America who resented her, the male golfers who felt she had no business playing in a men's field, the countless bloggers who called her spoiled and overrated, and just about everyone who didn't understand how she could possibly be worth so many millions of dollars before she was old enough to vote.

Wie parred 14, then hit a perfect drive to the corner of the dogleg left on the par-4 15th. More vehicles stopped along the highway; people got out of their cars to watch. On the way to her ball, Michelle saw the growing lineup of vehicles and laughed. Then she lofted a wedge shot that floated over a bunker and came to rest pin high, 7 feet from the cup. By now cars on the other side of the highway were stopping and people were getting out to follow the action. Some even stood on hoods. Wie's caddy, Greg Johnston, shook his head.

Wie made her 7-footer for birdie and accepted cheers from

the gallery—and the motorists—with a smile and a little wave. She could afford to smile. At 6 under par for the tournament with three holes left to play, she was going to make the cut with room to spare. A bogey on 16 made little difference. Wie made her final par putt on 18 to complete a round of 69, 3 under for the day, and a two-round total of 139. The cut was 144.

Michelle's parents did something as rare for them as B.J. sitting down on a golf course: they embraced in public. Usually B.J. and his wife, Bo, walked separately during Michelle's rounds. Now they were hugging. Bo whipped out a camera and started snapping pictures of everything, everyone, the whole happy scene. B.J. accepted handshakes and backslaps from relatives and strangers alike. His daughter was tied for 17th after two rounds.

The least excited person in the immediate vicinity appeared to be Michelle Wie. She smiled. She waved briefly. Her caddy put an arm around her in a half hug, and Wie leaned in against him slightly in appreciation. She walked to the scorer's tent, checked her card, signed it, and then made her way to the press room, signing autographs along the way. There she admitted, in Korean, to feeling "wonderful" and "really, really happy," but immediately added, "The tournament's not over yet."

The next day, Michelle spoke to a knot of reporters in the press room, this time in English. Outside, heavy rain washed out the day's round; she would finish the rain-shortened 54-hole event on Sunday in a tie for 35th place. But that would seem immaterial, given the history she'd already made.

"I think winning the Masters would be amazing," she said, unfolding big dreams, bigger than ever. "The craziest thing would be winning Player of the Year on the PGA Tour. These are ridiculous things, but that's what I'm here for, to do ridiculous things."

Asked if she really felt she could do everything she said she wanted to, Michelle Wie didn't hesitate:

"Definitely."

"It's not that difficult being me," she had remarked on that rainy May Saturday in South Korea when somebody asked about all the pressure she was under. "I have a pretty good life. I wouldn't change anything."

But Michelle Wie's golf life was about to change dramatically. In the six months to come, her dream of doing "ridiculous things" would give way to the reality of a career spiraling downward and out of control. Top 5 finishes in women's majors would give way to missed cuts and last-place horror stories. A surfeit of options about where to play next week would give way to fears about finding places to play next year.

And in the two years to come, leading up to the end of 2008, some of the same fans and media who'd had no doubt about her history-making future would begin to wonder if she had any golf future at all.

At this turning point in May 2006, as she made the cut in a men's professional golf tournament in South Korea, Michelle Wie made a case that someday—someday soon—she could compete on the PGA Tour. Two years later there was serious doubt whether she would qualify for the LPGA Tour.

What had gone wrong?

What happened to the "Next Tiger Woods"?

Would the teenage girl who gave us the opening chapters of one of the most thrilling stories in sports history give way to a young adult who would write a comeback story for the ages?

Barefoot Revolution

O n Monday, July 6, 1998, a 20-year-old woman got her feet wet and became a national hero in South Korea.

Se Ri Pak, an LPGA rookie from South Korea, who earlier in the year had won the LPGA Championship, and Jenny Chuasiriporn, also 20, a student at Duke University whose parents had emigrated from Thailand, faced off in a play-off for the 53rd U.S. Women's Open Championship. They had finished the first 72 holes on Sunday tied at 6-over-par 290. After a seesaw match on Monday, they came to the final hole of the 18-hole play-off tied at 1 over. There Pak made what appeared to be a fatal error when her drive on the 421-yard par 4 at Blackwolf Run in Kohler, Wisconsin, rolled through the left fairway into a water hazard.

Pak walked to the edge of the water, found her ball only partially submerged, and considered her options: take a drop and one-stroke penalty, or play it from the water and avoid the penalty stroke, gambling on moving the ball close enough to the green to get up and down. The first option was the safe play. The second was far riskier, because it could end with the ball still in the lake. Pak mulled her dilemma, then removed her shoes and socks and stepped into the water. The camera zeroed in on her feet, to show how deep she had to go, and revealed the stark tan line between leg and ankle, an image that would sear itself into millions of imaginations back in South Korea.

Her daring paid off. Pak made clean contact and moved the ball far enough up the fairway to leave her a wedge to the green. She dropped her next shot within 10 feet, then two-putted for a bogey. Chuasiriporn, who'd had her own troubles on the hole, couldn't get up and down for par from the edge of the green, so the match went to sudden death. On the second hole, Pak drained an 18-footer to become the youngest U.S. Women's Open Champion in history and a national hero in her native South Korea, where millions had watched the play-off on television. Many there knew little about golf and nothing about Se Ri Pak; now they were captivated and inspired.

The enduring symbol of that triumph, which launched an army of young women dedicated to following in Se Ri Pak's footsteps, was that tan line at her ankles, revealed to her countrymen on the day she made her bold choice—and made history. Pak went on to win three more majors and 24 more titles. She never lost in a play-off. Her work ethic has driven her to greatness, riches, and the World Golf Hall of Fame.

But she will always be remembered for that day and that shot.

Thousands of South Korean fathers saw that 1998 U.S. Open and rushed to model their daughters' lives after Pak's. And that is their generally accepted right in South Korea, where a still-strong strain of Confucianism insists the father is the head of the household both in actuality and in spirit. The Korean father is right even when he's wrong, so much so that if the Korean father is wrong, the world must be even more wrong.

Consider this summary in a Web page created by the Korean Cultural Center of Los Angeles: "Traditionally, the eldest male of a family was regarded as the source of supreme authority. All family members were expected to do what was ordered or desired by him. Strict instructions were to be obeyed without protest. It would have been unthinkable for children or grandchildren to place themselves in opposition to the wishes of their elders."

This sometimes leads to parental practices that in America would be considered tantamount to abuse. Se Ri Pak's father was a notoriously strict disciplinarian. When he learned his daughter feared graveyards, so legend has it, he made her sleep in one. He pushed her to practice so hard and so long in cold winter weather that by the time she was finally done she had icicles in her hair.

In America, these stories are horrifying. In South Korea, they are accepted as necessary steps in the making of a champion. "American parents are ignorant about their children's future," B.J. Wie's father, eighty-three-year-old Sang Kyu-Wie, once said. "They don't care."

One result is a stunning work ethic. A favored training technique of many South Koreans on the LPGA Tour is to tape sacks of sand to their ankles and walk briskly for half an hour or more to build leg strength—*after* hitting hundreds of balls on the range. Mi Hyun Kim, now 32 and a 10-year Tour veteran, once ventured out into the whipping wind of a tropical storm to play nine holes near her home in Orlando. She could barely stand up against the nearly hurricane-force winds, but she finished the nine holes.

After Pak's triumph, the rush turned into a stampede. Dozens of South Korean girls (and their parents) followed her to America, packing LPGA Tour leaderboards to such an extent that American golf writers sometimes made bets on tournaments, with one reporter taking the Lees and another taking the Kims. Koreans won a combined 11 Tour events in 2006 alone. In 2008, six of the Top 15 on the official money list were of South Korean descent. And more Lees and Kims are on the way. The largest two television contracts owned by the LPGA Tour are from Korean broadcasting companies.

Typically, Korean members of the LPGA Tour are quiet, reserved, and intense. *Very* intense. They don't crack jokes on the range or place $2 bets on the side during practice rounds. And even though Pak, now 31, has become somewhat Americanized—her English is excellent, and she says one of her goals is to "have fun"—she still burns inside. "If I leave the range before others," she says, "I feel lazy. Our country is so small. We work so hard. I feel pressure to work hard, to be good."

The pressure was great enough in Pak's rookie year to land her briefly in a South Korean hospital suffering from exhaustion. Michelle Wie had already been playing golf for four years when Se Ri Pak took her socks off on that summer day in 1998. And Michelle was born in America, not South Korea. But it's helpful to remember South Korea's story, and Pak's accomplishments, when trying to understand the course Wie's life took.

After all, B.J. and Bo Wie were both born in South Korea. They grew up as their country grew up. They found an identity as their nation found its own. And so even though they raised their only child in America, Michelle is very much a

Korean American. The language she speaks to her parents is Korean, or "Konglish," as she likes to say. And her family of three is extremely tight. They are each other's confidants, advisors, and best friends. Michelle sometimes even slept in her parents' bed as a young teen traveling on the mainland for tournaments.

"People who become murderers," Michelle said at age 13, "are people who don't spend enough time with their parents."

Holy Beauty

S he turned her head.

The newborn baby, just hours old, turned her head.

That was the first sign that Michelle Wie was special.

Most infants lie flat on their backs, swaddled in blankets, eyes searching the ceiling. They look so helpless. They are. But this girl named Sung-Mi Wie—the first two names mean "Holy Beauty" in Korean—swiveled her neck to look around. Almost as soon as she opened her eyes in that hospital on Oahu on October 11, 1989, she was in control, an athlete for sure.

She had long legs, a long torso, even a long neck. Her entire body stretched out 22 inches. She would grow to be pudgy at times, but never fat. Never overweight, except maybe at two weeks old, when she barely fit on the baby scale in the office of her Honolulu pediatrician. The doctor couldn't quite believe it: she was big even for a boy.

Sung-Mi Wie was strong, too. Ten days into her life, she found the power in her arms to push herself away from whatever was next to her. At two months, she rocked herself from her crib onto the floor. She was a force to be reckoned with before she could crawl.

She was adorable. With her bright, happy eyes, her tiny nose floating in the middle of her round face, and her wide crease of a smile, she almost looked like an emoticon. Such fragile features set against the backdrop of a large head, long limbs, big hands, and huge feet added the perfect touch of delicacy and grace to her oversized body. Her parents, now American citizens, gave her an American name, Michelle, after the Beatles song.

Most Korean parents want boys to carry on the family name. The Wies stopped with one child, a girl, their prize. They say they never wanted another, even though their daughter would grow to wish she had a brother or a sister to make practice more fun. To Michelle's parents, one was enough to give them a lifetime of happiness and awe. She was a holy beauty, and soon the entire world would know it.

The child's striking appearance made more sense when you saw her parents. Her dad, Byung-Wook, towers over most Korean men at 6'2". He has square shoulders, a Clark Kent jawline, and slightly wavy black hair. A soft, almost-tender voice belies his tirelessness, his certainty, and his temper. He, too, has an American name: B.J.

The last name traced back to the Tang Dynasty in China, around A.D. 675, which sent a group of scholars to the Korean peninsula to teach engineering. One of them was named Wie. Nearly a millennium later, in the late 1500s, the first of Wie's descendants settled in the small village of Changhung, 250 miles south of what is now Seoul. Michelle's grandfather still lives in Changhung today in a modest brown house next to a rice paddy, with a view of a mountain range and a highway that, like so much of modern-day South Korea, is brand-new.

This academic gene filtered down through the centuries to Michelle's great-grandfather, who was born in 1898 and taught Chinese. He raised a son who had a love for airplanes from the time he was a small child. Sang-Kyu Wie joined the Korean Air Force in 1951, just months after the outbreak of the Korean War. He flew 97 combat missions, often in American planes with American co-pilots, against the North Koreans and the Chinese. He won three U.S. medals, including a Distinguished Flying Cross. Hanging in the National Museum of the United States Air Force near Dayton, Ohio, is a painting of B.J.'s father in the cockpit of a propeller-driven plane, soaring low over a smoke-covered mountain range. The caption reads as follows:

WORKING TOGETHER TO DEFEND HILL 351

On March 26, 1952, sixteen F-51 Mustang fighter-bombers of the newly-created Republic of Korea Air Force (ROKAF) led by Maj. E. Yul Yoon furiously attacked communist ground forces attacking Hill 351. The air-to-ground action was being directed by a USAF T-6 Mosquito airborne forward air controller flown by Maj. William Light and ROKAF Capt. Sang K. Wie along with a USAF ground-based control party. During this action, US Navy aircraft and ROK Army artillery successfully suppressed enemy anti-aircraft fire. This joint action enabled the ROK 15th Infantry Division to effectively hold the strategic heights of Hill 351.

After the war, the young pilot returned home to his wife, Kyung-Hee. It was this woman, an inch taller than her husband and a descendant of North Koreans, who passed along her height and her strength to B.J. and then to Michelle. Together the couple traveled to the United States, where Sang-

Kyu became the first Korean to get an American Ph.D. in aerospace engineering, completing his studies at the University of Minnesota in 1959.

B.J.'s older brother, Bong, earned his doctorate in aeronautics and astronautics at Stanford and went on to become a rocket scientist—literally. He wrote a textbook entitled *Space Vehicle Dynamics and Control,* authored three U.S. patents, worked on half a dozen projects for NASA, and became a professor of mechanical and aerospace engineering at Arizona State University before taking a similar position at Iowa State.

B.J.'s sister, Bong Ae, also excelled in school and became a medical doctor in Seoul.

And B.J.?

"B.J. was not a genius," says Sang-Kyu. "He was okay. He was a nice boy."

Like everyone in his gifted family, the "nice boy" had a highly developed grasp of spatial logic and reasoning. He studied architecture at Hanyang University in Seoul and then took courses in city planning at Seoul National. He moved to America in 1983 to study urban planning at San Jose State, and then moved on to the University of Pennsylvania, where he earned his Ph.D. in transportation science.

Golf, with its swing planes, flight paths, aerodynamics, and slopes, melded perfectly with his academic interests; the golf course was an engineer's playground. But B.J. didn't find the sport on his own. That took the help of a beauty queen.

Hyun-Kyong Seo was also fairly tall (5'8"), with soft features, dark eyes, round cheeks, and a glowing smile. Miss Korea of 1985 had balance, poise, and a fair share of her family's athleticism. The family sport of preference was golf. Hyun-Kyong's mother, Maria, taught the game to her father, Joseph, and eventually they both played to single-digit handicaps. Hyun-Kyong—who would later take the nickname "Bo"—started playing in high school and eventually became an amateur champion in Korea.

And, like her mother before her, she introduced her husband to the game.

Bo first met B.J. when she was nine years old and he was a high school classmate of her brother. They were reunited in 1985 during Bo's reign as Miss Korea. After taking courses at a Korean branch of the University of Maryland, she left Seoul to study in California, where she had relatives. The two dated, played plenty of golf, and were married three years later.

B.J. and Bo played as often as they could in Seoul, but soon getting a tee time become a lot easier when B.J. landed a new job teaching transportation at the University of Hawaii at Manoa, a suburb of Honolulu. He and Bo found a one-bedroom apartment in a white brick tower near the main highway leading to downtown Honolulu, only a couple of exits from campus. From the fourteenth floor, the couple could see the hotel skyscrapers of Waikiki and the serenity of Pearl Harbor to the west.

But in 1989, the couple had to find a bigger place: a baby was on the way.

Michelle advanced rapidly in everything she did. Walked at nine months. Ran and chased tennis balls around B.J.'s office soon after. Ate almost as much at two and three as adults. Tried out for her elementary school baseball team when she was six and quickly became the squad's best hitter. The minute she picked up a tennis racquet, Michelle appeared ready to conquer that game, too, but she quit soon after she started because she didn't like to run. (B.J. once threw a can of tennis balls into a garbage can because he was so upset by his daughter's unwillingness to hurry after volleys.)

But one sport grabbed Michelle and didn't let go. She was four the day B.J. took her to Haha'ione Park in suburban Honolulu and walked her to a baseball field encircled by a low stone wall and a chain-link fence. He handed her one of her grandmother's clubs that he'd shortened so a four-year-old could swing it. She grabbed it with both hands, as if it were an ax, settled without prompting into a plausible golf stance with her pudgy legs shoulder width apart, and stared at the little white ball at her feet.

Michelle Wie poured everything her little body had into that first swipe. She felt the clubface meet its target, let the clubhead carry her arms around her body, and looked up to see the ball high in the Honolulu sky. B.J. watched as his daughter's drive soared, bounced, and rolled to rest deep in the outfield.

B.J. looked down at his little girl.

She gazed up at her father.

Michelle wanted to do it again.

From the first, Michelle just flat out loved crushing a golf ball. She threw her entire body into the game, sliding her coiled legs through the downswing as if she were moving a couch. In no time, the heroes in the Wie household were the golf pros with the best swings. Michelle had a poster of Tiger Woods in her room, and B.J. carried around a photo of him in midswing so he could refer to it anytime his daughter needed help.

Michelle watched both the PGA Tour and the LPGA Tour on television, but she loved the big hitters on the men's side more than the finesse players on the women's. As she sat in front of her parents' TV at age six, nothing about her dreams seemed the least bit strange. After all, her mother had once shot a 69 in Maui and won an amateur tournament back in Seoul.

Why shouldn't she aim higher?

Neither mother nor father put any limits on their daughter's dreams and ambitions. They encouraged her every swing, her desire to hit longer, longer, longer. And that's just what she did.

But Michelle's determination to measure her talent against others sparked a backlash the moment she started playing on municipal links. When she was seven, her parents walked her to the first tee at a local course and the starter asked Michelle for her age. She gave it. "Sorry," he said, shaking his head. "Too young."

Michelle was stunned. "What I really wanted to tell him," she said later, "was, 'I can beat you!' "

The starter finally relented. He paired Michelle with a single-handicapper; the older woman wasn't pleased. Michelle, full of fire, airmailed her drives past her reluctant playing partner. She birdied a 200-yard par 3. The woman left the course after nine holes.

By age nine, Michelle was beating her parents, who gave up their own games to mentor her. With no course within walking distance of their home, they drove east about fifteen minutes along the Kalanianaole Highway, which curls along seaside cliffs and then up and around a mountain range, to the Olomana Golf Links, a public course in Waimanalo. There they went to the top shelf of a bilevel driving range, where Michelle pounded away until, one day, B.J. went downstairs looking for the head pro.

Casey Nakama was born in Honolulu in 1958. Athletic as a kid, he played shooting guard in high school but soon realized he was too short for basketball. He picked up golf in 1976, won an Oahu amateur tournament three straight years, and turned pro in 1985.

Nakama went on to play on the Asian Tour and made the Hogan Tour back in the States, but struggled and returned to Hawaii to teach. He started at Olomana with adults; then a parent asked him to teach juniors in 1996. Tiger Woods turned pro the next year, and suddenly dozens of kids showed up at Nakama's door.

A few years later, he spotted a tall girl whaling away, spraying her shots everywhere and not seeming to care. He saw the potential right away—the 10-year-old Wie was more than 5' tall already—but there were problems. "She could carry the ball 200 yards," Nakama said. "But the only thing she had going for her was her size. Her swing plane was flat and laid-off. Her short game was really bad. She didn't know what she was doing."

Yet Michelle had inherited another important family trait: her intelligence. She could recite the alphabet at one and started reading at two, even though her parents spoke to her in Korean and sometimes struggled to find the right word in English. She was accepted at the top academy in Hawaii, the elite Punahou School, founded in 1841 by missionaries and now the largest independent school on one campus in the United States. Wie applied as a rising sixth grader, enrolled, and earned mostly A's throughout her stay there.

But her greatest gift was her ability to learn visually, almost photographically. She could burn through her homework during the forty-minute drive to Olomana. She could receive a swing lesson and incorporate what she learned almost immediately. Then, somehow, she could lock in the motion and not stray from it.

Nakama went to work, telling Michelle to point the club

toward the target at the top of her backswing, hinge her wrists, and make sure her top two knuckles pointed upward when she gripped the club. Michelle would watch herself in the huge wall mirror outside his office and practice until dark. Once she got home, she practiced some more. "After a couple days," Nakama said, "she would come back and say, 'Casey! I think I got it!' "

And she had: gradually Michelle's spray became a sweet draw, and she started chaining perfect shot after perfect shot.

In 2000, Michelle won the girls' division of the Oahu Junior Championship. Newspapers love young achievers—Honolulu feels more like an extended family than a big city—so few reporters dampened the achievement by harping on the fact that Oahu had very few girl golfers. All that mattered was that a tall-for-her-age 10-year-old had won despite plunking three shots in the water.

She never tired of practicing. "It didn't bother her to work on her swing five or six days a week," Nakama said. "I remember one Halloween night, my wife and I had just gotten a puppy. I asked Michelle, 'Are you going to go trick-or-treating?' She said no. Instead she went to her dad to ask, 'If I stay and practice, can I play with the puppy?' It was borderline sad."

The Wie family tolerated no laziness. From the moment B.J. realized his daughter had talent, there would be no letting up. Michelle had the engine, ignited by her mother's love for the game, but B.J. did the steering and stepped on the gas. His daughter reported to Olomana after school every day to follow the same drill: practice at the range, play nine holes, then chip. "Her dad was in control of everything," Nakama said. "He was always pressing, pressing, pressing for more. Never rude, but always pressing."

Nakama noticed early on that B.J. didn't know the game as well as he let on. "It was kind of hilarious to see him on the greens," Nakama says. "He didn't know what he was looking at. It was comical." B.J. allegedly played to a two-handicap, yet Michelle chipped with her hands straight out instead of flexed. When Nakama showed her the right way, Michelle turned to her dad and said, "See, I told you I was doing it wrong!"

He doesn't know how to play golf, Nakama said to himself.

Yet B.J. kept pressing for improvement, for more work, for smarter application of the lessons. His expectations were sky-high not only for himself and for Michelle but also for everyone else around him.

"Everything hinged on Mr. Wie," Nakama said later. "He was brutal."

Michelle leapt from lesson to lesson, and soon Nakama suggested a local USGA qualifier for the Women's Amateur Public Links to see how Wie measured against other girls her age. Wie took her grandmother's clubs to a pretty Oahu course named Alawai and shot an 80, tying for the last available qualifying spot for the national stage in North Carolina. She won the play-off with a par on the first hole, and suddenly she and her parents were on a plane heading to the mainland.

Michelle Wie made her media debut on June 30, 2000, in the *Honolulu Advertiser.* The *Advertiser* reported that Wie was the youngest player ever to qualify for the Women's Amateur Public Links. A writer from the Associated Press asked how she felt playing against so many older girls and young women. "I just think about my game," she said. "I don't really think about other people."

She teed off against competitors 10 years or more her senior, and she outdrove most of them, making the turn on her first day at a stunning 1-under 35. She finished with an incredible 74. The next day, Wie's score rose to 6 over before weather pushed everyone off the North Carolina course. She cried from frustration through much of the round. Still, she was about to make the match play stage as the youngest person ever to play for a USGA title. Yet she never showed a trace of anxiety.

"I don't feel scared or nervous," she would say a few years later. "Just butterflies. They go away after the first shot."

The following day, July 5, the *Charlotte Observer* picked up on the story, saying that Wie was "taking the youth movement to a new extreme." Days later, *Boston Globe* reporter Jim McCabe offered the first newspaper comment on Wie when he wrote: "Ten years old! I have dirt on my clubs older than that!" But Wie made history, losing in match play to 24-year-old Cindy Lee of Tempe, Arizona. "When I was ten," Lee said, "I was playing piano or something."

No one knew quite what to make of this girl.

By age 11, Wie had run out of female competition at home. She was the youngest to win the Hawaii Women's Stroke Play Championship. "She had blown everyone away," said Sean Lunasco, cofounder and Webmaster of local golf site 808golf.com. "So B.J. would look toward the male side. He was only doing that to get her more competition."

Nakama agrees: "It was strictly for competition. There were only two or three women's tournaments in a year."

Yet that didn't go over too well in Honolulu, or anywhere else in the state. Locals dismissed the *wahine*—girl—as not belonging in men's tournaments. Some tournament directors simply told B.J. flat out to take his daughter elsewhere.

Nakama worried about backlash. "Whether you know it or not," he told B.J., "you are insulting the women on the LPGA."

B.J. replied: "I don't think so. I think it's a good thing. A lot of women are behind us."

Nakama nodded. "Just be careful."

But B.J. never unmade a choice, and Michelle never hesitated on the course. She grew to be 5'11", with braces, by age 12. She was afraid of getting her ears pierced, afraid of clowns, and afraid of the dark. But she was not afraid of playing against men.

Tommy Kim, a Hawaii state long-drive champion, remembers being in the group ahead of Wie when she became the first female to play in the State Open in Maui. "This guy I was playing with was a decent golfer," Kim said, "and he was talking to his buddy, 'I'm not going to let her outdrive me.' She not only outdrove him, she beat him by 20 strokes."

Michelle made the cut and finished in a tie for 17th overall. Nakama says he thought, *Wow! She might be able to compete here against men all the time.*

B.J. began trying to crack Hawaii's tight-knit and powerful golf community. He made friends with three women who would become Michelle's "aunties": Bev Kim, winner of golf titles in five different decades and a member of the Hawaii Golf Hall of Fame; Lily Yao, vice chairwoman of the First Hawaiian Bank; and Linda Johnston, a top Oahu Realtor. Kim was good friends with *Honolulu Advertiser* writer Ann Miller and reminded Miller frequently of Wie's promise.

Yao was so impressed with Wie that she started a foundation for junior golfers in Hawaii. "She's such a polite, well-mannered young lady," said Yao. "The whole family is so well-mannered and courteous and humble." Yao persuaded an officer of a major accounting firm to set up the foundation pro bono. Yao and Johnston then went into the community and raised $70,000 for the new foundation; Yao turned her 60th birthday into a fund-raiser and added another $187,000. Michelle was the first recipient of a check.

"Linda and I gave Michelle personal financial support annually until she turned pro," says Yao. "It wasn't big money, but it was support when the Wies needed it." Yao, who was also chairperson of the Honolulu Chamber of Commerce, found other donors to the Wie cause, and even went to a high-ranking friend at United Airlines and got some help with tickets for the Wies to travel to mainland tournaments. "We are so proud of her," Yao said. "We want to capture her as a representative for Hawaii."

B.J. came to Yao in 2001 and asked for help in getting Michelle a sponsor's exemption to the LPGA Takefuji Classic, scheduled to be played on Oahu. The answer was no: Michelle would have to wait a year and then qualify for her first LPGA tournament—which, the following year, she did.

"The whole family is very goal-oriented," Yao said. "They plan step by step to achieve what they want. They are super marketers. They do a lot of research, and as a professor at the university, B.J. knows how to get information. They knew how to contact the right people."

As driven as he was in managing Michelle's budding career, B.J.—unlike so many other golf parents—never scolded Michelle for poor shots. He simply stood close by on the practice range, holding a few range balls, dropping another as soon as Michelle hit one. He might advise on alignment or posture, but he mostly just watched and helped.

"I never saw him mad at her," Nakama says. "He was never negative. That was amazing."

Ty Votaw, former commissioner of the LPGA (1999–2005), remembers the first time he laid eyes on Michelle Wie. It was on a driving range at the Takefuji Classic in 2002, after Wie became the youngest golfer ever to qualify for an LPGA Tour event. Votaw saw her from a distance and thought she was 25.

Wie missed the cut by only three strokes. She beat dozens of women professionals. "I'm just happy to be here," she said to the press afterward. "There's free food and free drinks and nobody bothers you on the practice greens."

She went on to play in two more LPGA Tour tournaments that year, and she became the youngest ever to advance to the semifinals of the Women's Amateur Public Links Championship.

Annika Sorenstam met Wie for the first time at Takefuji that year and asked her what her handicap was. Wie said she didn't have one. Sorenstam, the greatest female golfer of all time, didn't know what to say. She herself didn't even play seriously until she was 14.

This 12-year-old girl had already made six holes in one.

Big Wiesy

Michelle Wie's life changed forever in January 2002, with just one swing of her driver. The swing reverberated around the world, and in some ways it still does.

For four years beginning in 2002, the Waialae Country Club hosted a six-hole alternate-ball Pro-Junior Challenge on the Tuesday before the PGA Tour's Sony Open in January. It included six pros and six local juniors. The event was put on by First Hawaiian Bank, where Michelle Wie's "auntie," Lily Yao, served as vice chairperson. The inaugural version included Fred Couples, Tom Lehman, Davis Love III, and Scott Simpson. A pro at the country club named Greg Nichols served as emcee and conducted what is believed to be the first televised interview with Wie. The 12-year-old told Nichols, and the camera, that she wanted to play in the Masters.

"It was her dream to be famous," Nichols recalls. "Maybe

it would be softball or tennis, not necessarily golf, but famous. She had big, dreamy stars in her eyes."

Nichols became friends with the Wie family and eventually saw them frequently at the new Ko Olina Golf Resort across the island, where he took a job as general manager later that same year. Michelle practiced there often, even though the drive from the family condo took her parents a half hour or more. "To this day," Nichols said in 2007, "I've never seen Michelle without her mom and dad."

But while B.J. encouraged Michelle all the way, Nichols says, "it was her idea, her dream, to compete against men, not his. He took it and ran with it, but the idea did not come from him. If anything, B.J.'s mistake was allowing Michelle to have her way."

The 12 players assembled on the first tee for a group photo and then teed off. Michelle was paired with Tom Lehman, and they followed Scott Simpson and his amateur partner. She planted her feet, stared down at the ball, and coiled into a swing that the pros had not seen. Her ball rocketed off the tee. The pros' heads snapped up and out toward the horizon, their eyes locked on its flight. Michelle's drive landed and rolled to within a step or two of Simpson's ball.

Davis Love III called it "one of the best golf swings I've ever seen, period."

Couples chimed in: "When you see her hit a golf ball . . . well, there's nothing that prepares you for it. It's just the scariest thing you've ever seen."

Lehman took just one look at the swing and saw a parallel with the fluid rhythm of Ernie Els, aka "Big Easy." And that's how Michelle got a new nickname: "Big Wiesy."

Gary Gilchrist, 44, is a ruddy-faced South African who looks like Els' shorter cousin. Today, Gilchrist is a walking encyclopedia of girls' junior golf. But back in the mid-1990s, when the South African moved from Texas to Florida to work for master teacher David Leadbetter, he was only just venturing into a remote corner of the golf world: teaching the game to young girls.

"It wasn't cool at all for girls to play golf back then," he says. "Annika Sorenstam was very hard to relate to in the junior game."

But Gilchrist took a handful of kids under his wing, and in less than a decade he led the way in the building of a small army of young women who now rival their tennis counterparts in fame and visibility.

As a scratch golfer as a teenager growing up in Durban, Gilchrist earned a spot on the South African national team before going into military service. Upon his release, he turned pro, earned his card on the South Africa Tour, and played for four years before he saw the handwriting on the wall: he wasn't the next Gary Player.

So Gilchrist went to work as an instructor at the Leadbetter Academy in Bradenton, Florida. Part of his job was to scour the country, relying on a pair of eyes that had seen some of the world's best male players, looking for new talent. Female talent.

His first big find was a freckle-faced, ponytailed 13-year-old from Pleasanton, California, named Paula Creamer. Gilchrist persuaded Creamer and her parents, Paul and Karen, to relocate to Florida so their daughter could enroll in the Leadbetter Academy. Paula had a mental edge rarely seen in girls her age. (Or boys, for that matter.) On the course, a sunshiny smile turned into a near sneer when she bore down. She was called "Pink Panther" because of her love for the color, but the nickname also fit because she was downright predatory in competition. In time, Creamer would become the leader of a generation of juniors that altered women's golf, and Gilchrist was right by her side from the start.

Then, late in 2002, when Paula was 16, her dad got a call from her coach. Gilchrist knew Paul Creamer wanted his daughter to be the only supernova in golf's new galaxy, but the coach felt his job was to find and develop talent. And he believed Paula would benefit from the competition, of which there was very little at the time.

"I found a girl," Gilchrist blurted, a current of excitement in his voice. "She's gonna compete against Paula her entire life." Paul Creamer held the phone in his hand for a moment and said nothing. Gilchrist knew this wasn't welcome news. He offered another bit of information: "She's 12."

Gilchrist didn't much care about Creamer's concerns, not at that point. He had heard of this phenom in Hawaii, and he knew he had to check her out for himself. So he flew there to meet the Wies. There, over lunch near a local driving range, he was impressed with what he found. "The family bond was tremendously strong," he says. "And they talked to her like she was an adult."

Gilchrist's philosophy with young golfers, he says, is simple: find out what they want to do and help them do it. Michelle and Bo sat silently while B.J. spoke about his daughter's game, and as soon as Gilchrist got the chance, he asked Michelle what she wanted to do with her game. She answered quickly: "I want to play in the Masters."

B.J. looked at his daughter, then back at Gilchrist, and beamed.

"He laughed a little," Gilchrist says. "But it wasn't a nervous laugh."

The foursome walked to the range, where Michelle took out a seven-degree Fujikura driver and set up a ball. At least a dozen people stood around, watching. Some of them had seen her hit a golf ball before, and they knew what to expect. Gilchrist looked for a trace of nerves, a sense of anxiety at the challenge of performing for a golf expert from the mainland and a small crowd of onlookers. He saw none.

Michelle pulled the clubhead away from the ball, swept it back in a long arc, and brought it down and through in a fluid, powerful motion that ended with it high and behind her left shoulder. Gilchrist watched the ball take flight, let his eye drop to the last target on the range—a 230-yard marker—then watched the ball sail over the marker. He felt a visceral rush.

"I had never seen any boy her age swing a club like that, much less a girl," he recalled. "The control. The fluidity. The power. And it was all natural."

Michelle proceeded to crush rocket after rocket. She didn't seem to care if the ball went left or right as long as it went far. She seemed addicted to the sound, the power, and the distance. And it seemed like she wasn't even trying. Michelle Wie had a perfect golf swing at the age of 12.

How was that possible?

Gilchrist thought of what he had just seen and was thrilled that he had found her before anyone else. "I just sat there listening and watching," he would write in his notes, "wondering if this was all real." Gilchrist was left with only one slight concern. "When I met Paula, she wanted to be the number one golfer in the world," he said. "I don't think winning was everything to Michelle. She just loved hitting the ball."

Casey Nakama found out about the Leadbetter Academy representative's meeting with the Wies by reading about it in the paper. He knew Michelle would eventually move on to a place with better facilities and a bigger name. So he waited for B.J. to give him the bad news. But Michelle's father didn't, not right away. Eventually Nakama asked to speak with him privately.

At their meeting, Nakama learned that the decision had been made: Michelle would be working under Gilchrist's tutelage. Nakama understood. But he wondered where Michelle would practice. She couldn't stay at Olomana, could she? Wouldn't that be using facilities without giving anything in return? Nakama went to the club owner to lobby on her behalf only to learn that B.J. had already met with him to request permission to play without membership or dues.

"He didn't have to go behind my back," Nakama says. "If he'd had any balls, he'd have told me not to bother. It would have been fine. But he slides around."

Gilchrist had his own ties to cut. The Wies wanted him as Michelle's full-time coach. He had to call the Creamers and let them know that their coach and confidant had cast his lot with a younger, less tested golfer. "Paula felt like I betrayed her," he says. It was a decision Gilchrist would mull over until this day.

And yet the coach could not dwell too much on what he had given up. He had found a teenager he thought had the chance to become the greatest female golfer in history. Michelle Wie made everyone around her imagine the future. Gilchrist says he thought she could win a major by the age of 16 "easily," even though no one younger than 18 had ever won a tournament of any sort on the LPGA Tour. He also figured that if Wie got to the Masters at *any* age, she'd be worth $100 million.

Over the next few years, Gilchrist became very close with the family, traveling the nation with them mostly by minivan. He'd watch as B.J. charted the slope of every single green and jotted notes and arrows in the book he carried as Michelle's caddy. But Gilchrist became wary of B.J. Wie's obsessive desire to control every aspect of the game. To Gilchrist, success at golf meant accepting that things will go wrong. To B.J., Gilchrist says, there was an answer for everything: "There was too much emphasis on being perfect."

Bo was equally driven. She was organized and detail-oriented. She watched every putt, raked every trap, carried the rain gear, and fed Michelle with fruit and water (along with a special concoction made from ginseng and deer antler to aid her energy and digestion). "The mom has a great eye," Gilchrist discovered quickly, "and if she saw something that wasn't right, she wanted to tell her right then."

"A lot of people complained from the beginning about her parents being on top of her on every shot," says Tommy Kim, a Hawaii-born pro and state long drive champ who practiced with Michelle on Oahu. "Her dad would stand within two feet, like he was going to get hit. Guys were like, 'Give her some room to breathe.' "

Although there were moments when Kim and Michelle talked, the parents were always right there to make sure it wasn't a buddy-buddy thing: "Michelle was there to work—period. If she was wandering away, the dad would always be there to pull her back. We'd try to invite her to play but it was hard to get her on the phone. It seemed like a one-sided thing. We were there to help her along, not to be her friends."

B.J. wasn't about to back off, not one little bit. "B.J. and Bo love her more than anything in the world," says longtime family friend and Hawaii State Junior Golf Association founder Mary Bea Porter-King. "Whether you agree with them or not, they are with her every step. They live and die with every shot."

And she adds: "There's nothing harder than watching your own child perform."

Michelle's parents rarely walked the course in tandem. Bo would hurry ahead to the spot where she thought her daughter's drives would land. Deeply religious, she would sometimes stand along the ropes and pray. She smiled politely at those she knew but rarely initiated conversation. A jumble of emotions, she often looked as if she sensed trouble.

B.J. was the polar opposite. He usually looked like things were going great, or were about to shift in that direction. Bo, afraid to test her English in public, remained a mystery to outsiders. The outgoing B.J. seemed perfectly happy to talk with the media. Bo appeared embarrassed by all the attention; B.J. asked Gilchrist for advice on how to make the most of the publicity (but wouldn't take Gilchrist's suggestion about consulting a PR specialist). As often as he could get to a computer, B.J. Googled news stories about his daughter. And instead of hiring a caddy, B.J. carried her bag himself. Looping for her gave him a perfect vantage point and a perfect opportunity to advise her on every shot.

The family's closeness rankled some onlookers almost as soon as the group hit the mainland for the 2003 season. While Tiger Woods' dad often stayed dozens or even hundreds of yards away from his son during tournaments, the Wies stood as close to their daughter as possible. When he wasn't on her bag, B.J. always had his binoculars at the ready—"G'shot, 'chelle!" he would cheer again and again—and Bo's yells of "Yesss!" after made putts became hallmarks of a Michelle Wie round in a tournament.

"The more the parent is seen, the more people dislike the child," says Gilchrist. "The fewer comments he makes, the easier it's going to be for her. But it's been difficult for them to stay out of it."

And B.J. was only going to get closer.

The first major on the LPGA Tour calendar takes place every spring in Rancho Mirage, California. It's officially entitled the Kraft Nabisco Championship, but it's still better known, to older fans and golfers alike, as the Dinah Shore. Either way, the tournament is celebrated for allowing amateurs to compete, so it seemed natural in 2003 to invite the young curiosity from Hawaii. Most teens who got a shot at the Kraft Nabisco played their two rounds, took some interview requests from hometown papers, missed the cut, and went home with some pictures and memories.

Not Michelle Wie.

Wie was paired in the first round with two young players who would soon become big names on the LPGA Tour: Christina Kim and Natalie Gulbis. Kim, a Korean American like Wie, is loud and outspoken and endlessly charming. Gulbis is so attractive that people routinely overlook her talent and gregarious personality. She would go on to become a pinup girl and a regular date of NFL star Ben Roethlisberger.

But back in 2003, all three just wanted to make the cut. Early in the tournament, Wie asked Gulbis if she could swap her 1 ball for a 2 ball. Gulbis deadpanned, "We don't allow that on this tour." Wie looked like she was about to cry as she glanced over at Kim for help. She shrugged, and Wie warbled that she didn't have another 1 ball. Gulbis finally let her in on the joke—the swap was okay—and all three laughed. They became friends.

Meanwhile, Gilchrist paid more attention to the reaction to Wie. He watched other caddies gasp for breath when the 13-year-old vaporized a drive. He noticed even the stoic Annika Sorenstam smiling incredulously at the stunning distance the girl covered. By the end of the weekend, Sorenstam would get the best view of anyone: Wie tied an amateur record by shooting a 66 in the third round and wound up in the final group on Sunday, teeing off alongside Sorenstam.

Wie finished tied for ninth, and couldn't accept prize money because of her amateur status, but she had won the day and the weekend. When she walked to the final green, crossing the bridge over the famous pond where winners traditionally plunge in celebration, the gallery screamed and applauded. It was that March Sunday in 2003 when the larger golf world beyond Hawaii first learned the name Michelle Wie.

And yet the next great thing in women's golf that season wasn't Michelle Wie but a 21-year-old dynamo named Virada Nirapathpongporn, who'd won the NCAA women's individual championship at Duke in 2002.

"Oui"—the nickname came from a relative when she was a child—arrived at the Women's Amateur Public Links Championship in June 2003 and blazed through the Publinx bracket and made the finals. Her opponent: Michelle Wie.

"If you just look at her face, you go, 'Okay, she's a kid,' " Nirapathpongporn said in an interview in response to a question about her younger opponent. "But then you look at her physique, and it's 'Wow!' "

Oui and Wie met in the 36-hole final at Ocean Hammock, outside of Daytona Beach. Typically, only a few dozen spectators show up for an amateur tournament consisting mostly of college girls and young women. But on this day, hundreds turned out for a showdown between a 21-year-old force and a 13-year-old prodigy.

At officially sanctioned junior events, the USGA doesn't allow parents to caddy for their offspring. "It's better not to have the parent involved," explains USGA rules official Marty Parkes. "We've seen too many incidents. The burden of suspicion falls on them." But this wasn't a junior event, and the USGA placed no such restriction, so B.J. Wie carried his daughter's clubs.

One of Oui's Duke buddies, Andy Dawson, carried her bag, and later told a reporter what he remembered about the first time he ever saw Michelle Wie swing a golf club: "It was amazing. The sound her clubhead made on contact, if you closed your eyes, it sounded like that of a male pro. I'd never seen a woman hit it anywhere like that, much less a young girl. She had it all."

To counter Wie's power, Oui had a killer short game. The Bangkok-born Nirapathpongporn came out blistering, making putts long and short, and forcing many along the ropes to wonder if the much younger Wie even had a chance. After eight holes, Nirapathpongporn led her young opponent 4 up. It was going to be a rout.

"At that point," says Dawson, "I'd have put Virada up against any woman in the game. She was the NCAA champion. She was the toughest player Michelle Wie had ever played. I'd have bet big money that Michelle would have withered away."

He'd have lost that bet.

Wie birdied three of the next five holes to cut the lead to 1. As the round went on, Michelle and her caddy-father conducted a little sideshow, with animated exchanges in Korean. Frequently, Michelle's teenage petulance clashed with B.J.'s attempt to assist and inform . . . and control. Korean parents have a reputation in junior golf as drill sergeants, and their daughters usually responded meekly and submissively. Michelle was every bit as opinionated and stubborn as her "Ap-ba." "We were always arguing," Michelle told *The New York Times* later that year, "but I was always right."

She was also impatient. After drives, Michelle quickly strode down the course, past Nirapathpongporn's ball, sometimes until she and her father stood in the fairway and in the opponent's line of sight. Dawson had seen the worst of parental behavior as a director of tournament operations for the American Junior Golf Association. He'd seen parents scream and behave poorly enough to warrant banishment from the course. B.J. came nowhere near that kind of behavior, but Dawson firmly told the older man to move.

"He'd walk up and stand in the middle of the fairway," says Dawson. "Maliciously? I don't know. It was like he was trying to intimidate us, and I didn't appreciate it."

The battle between Wie and Oui went on, back and forth, with Oui holding her lead but losing steam. "I was running out of gas," Nirapathpongporn says. Then, on the 24th hole, a par 5, Wie flew a sand shot over a water hazard and onto the green. It was one of several risks she took that day, and one of several times she ignored her father's advice. She made birdie and squared the match.

Finally, on the 34th hole, up 1, Wie stepped to the tee and faced a tough decision to make on the par 4 that bent left around a large pond. Play it safe, or cut the corner and hope to get home in 2? Wie didn't need to take the risk, but she took it anyway. She lit into her drive and watched it sail 250, 270, 280 yards . . . slightly left, then a bit more. But it looked to be just far enough, and it landed on the far bank. It was dry.

Then her ball slowly rolled back down the side of the bank and disappeared into the water.

USGA rules call for the drop point of a ball that goes into a water hazard to be behind the point where it crossed over the water. But B.J. strode all the way up to the bank where the ball landed and indicated that his daughter would take her drop from there.

Nirapathpongporn just stared. "I knew when Michelle's dad went way up, I knew it wasn't that far up," she said afterward. "I don't like to confront people on things like that, so I let my caddy take care of it."

Dawson burned: "He's an overzealous dad, and he's very proud and protective of his daughter. At the time he hadn't learned as much about golf as he thought he knew. She hit it into the water. It didn't cross. It carried over the water before hitting the far bank. Open and shut. But B.J. kind of threw a hissy fit. He was way out of line."

The two summoned USGA rules officials, almost a half dozen in all, and continued to argue. B.J. wouldn't back down. Nirapathpongporn worried a fight would break out. It didn't. In the end, B.J. capitulated, and Michelle dropped a ball back by the tee. She lost the hole.

The match was even, with two holes to play.

On the next-to-last hole, a par 3 over water, Michelle two-putted, then watched as Nirapathpongporn eyeballed her 3-footer to halve the hole. Michelle reached down into her pocket, her fingers searching for something she had left in there: a lucky coin. She grasped it. And she prayed that Nirapath-pongporn would miss.

Virada tapped the ball. It lipped out. Michelle let go of the coin. She was 1 up going into the last hole.

A few years later, when *Golf Digest* asked Michelle for a secret from her past, she mentioned her prayer. She hadn't forgiven herself. But Nirapathpongporn did. "If I were that young," she laughed when she heard about it, "I'd have done the same thing."

On the final hole, they both made par—no drama this time—and it was over. At 13, Michelle Wie had beaten a 21-year-old star to become the youngest girl ever to win a USGA event. Her reaction was telling. She didn't cry, hop up and down in glee, or high-five everybody in sight. More than anything else, she seemed overcome by relief. Said Dawson: "I don't think she realized what she'd just done."

Everyone else did. After her top-10 performance at the Kraft Nabisco earlier in the year and now the win against a NCAA champion, there seemed no limit to Wie's future. "For those people who don't like how Michelle gets so much attention," Nirapathpongporn would say two years later, "I take blame for the birth of Michelle Wie. Sorry, world!"

But no one else was sorry. Wie ushered in an excitement about the future of women's golf that had never before existed, even in the era of the popular and charismatic Nancy Lopez. Wie was her sport's Tracy Austin.

Over the next few weeks B.J.'s cell phone rang incessantly. He got calls from ABC's *World News Tonight, NBC Nightly News,* CNN, ESPN, BBC, Greta Van Susteren, Bryant Gumbel, the *Today* show, *60 Minutes, Best Damn Sports Show, People, Sports Illustrated, YM, Teen Vogue, Glamour, Late Show with David Letterman, The Tonight Show with Jay Leno,* countless major newspapers, and even more Asian media outlets. A friend from Tokyo even called to inform B.J. that his daughter was now the second most popular athlete in Japan.

Tiger Woods was 15 when he won his first national championship. Jack Nicklaus was 17. Nancy Lopez was 15. Mickey Wright was 17. Babe Didrikson Zaharias didn't even start playing golf until she was 24.

Michelle Wie was a national champion at 13.

Only a few weeks later, she headed to Oregon for the biggest event in women's golf: the U.S. Women's Open. A 13-year-old had a chance to become the youngest woman ever to make the U.S. Open cut.

It seemed like the perfect pairing at the time. Eighteen years earlier, when she was 19, LPGA veteran Danielle Ammaccapane had won the U.S. Women's Public Links title, so for the first two rounds of the 2003 Open, the USGA paired her with the current Publinx champ.

Problem was, Ammaccapane had little patience for distractions, and Wie was only one of many at the Pumpkin Ridge

Golf Club in Oregon that July 4 weekend. A record 14 teenagers (including Paula Creamer and Morgan Pressel) qualified. For this one weekend, the most prestigious tournament in women's golf had become, for better and worse, amateur hour. And Danielle Ammaccapane found herself paired with the star of the show.

From the start, Ammaccapane seemed perturbed. After a perfunctory greeting on the first tee, she said little to Wie. An official who walked with the pair described the tone of the day as "frosty." And relations weren't improved any by the behavior of Michelle's caddy, B.J. Wie.

As he had at the Publinx, B.J. strode rapidly ahead after the golfers finished their tee shots. Fine; Michelle had been penalized two strokes for slow play at an earlier LPGA Tour event, and he wanted to be sure that didn't happen again. But he evidently didn't pay close attention to where he stood when he got to Michelle's tee ball, which always lay well ahead of Ammaccapane's, and within a few holes the pro was steamed. Professional golfers aren't accustomed to having caddies or other players in their line of vision as they line up a shot. Course etiquette mandates that a golfer and her caddy stand well to the side until the short hitter makes her shot. Maybe B.J. didn't know this. On the first three driving holes, Ammaccapane's caddy had to wave B.J. and Michelle to the side. Maybe B.J. was a slow learner.

Ammaccapane got even more upset on the 14th green (they'd started on 10) when Michelle walked on Ammaccapane's extended putting line. The pro piped up, testily pointing out the faux pas.

It was all downhill from there.

Later in the round, Ammaccapane pulled her drive deep into the left rough, while Wie pushed hers right. Ammaccapane arrived at her ball, sized it up, and addressed it. But as she came through on her downswing, she heard a thwack from the other side of the fairway. Wie had hit her approach at the exact same time, even though etiquette demands that the longer driver hit last. Ammaccapane's shot landed in the bunker.

"She was not amused," said Marty Parkes, then USGA communications director, who walked the course with the group that day. "I felt it was totally inadvertent. But Danielle was not at all pleased."

Ammaccapane saved par, but it didn't matter. She was livid. "The worst was the father," she later told *Golf Digest*. "He wouldn't get pins, couldn't rake a bunker right, kept leaving the bag in the putting line, let his player putt with the flag in. I'm trying to play in the U.S. Open, and I've got Dumb and Dumber over here." Tracy Hanson, the third player in the group, later confirmed Ammaccapane's evaluation of B.J. in the same *Golf Digest* article, adding that B.J. "doesn't know how to be a proper caddy, and tends to over-celebrate."

At the end of the round, Parkes said, "You could tell there was a lot of tension there." Ammaccapane refused to shake the 13-year-old's hand on the final green. In golf, nothing sends a message quite like that.

Michelle was dazed. She didn't know what to think. She'd grown up surrounded by enthusiastic fans and well-wishers, and she could hardly fathom jealousy, let alone brush it off. Now a woman old enough to be her mother was angrier with her than Bo had ever been. And the situation would only sour.

After the round, Ammaccapane approached Wie in the scorer's tent. Their eyes met. Then Ammaccapane said something that Michelle says she will never forget: "You are the worst kid I have ever seen playing golf. You will never make it playing this game." (Ammaccapane's version, as reported in *Golf Digest,* went like this: "Michelle, that was the worst etiquette I've ever seen. If you want to be out here, you need to do better.")

Whatever the exact words were, Wie froze.

Reporters who had been following the group had picked up on the tension. B.J. greeted one he knew and mentioned something Michelle told him, that Ammaccapane had brushed his daughter on the way off the course. But something got lost in translation at some point between Michelle and B.J. and the reporter's notebook: "brushed" became "bumped."

B.J. saw the coverage the next morning and winced: he immediately fired himself as caddy and vowed to correct the reporting error as soon as he got to the course. By then it was too late. As the Wies approached the clubhouse, they noticed an elderly man standing at the entrance. It was no one they knew, so they kept on walking toward the door. Then the man stepped forward and blocked the entrance. It was Ammaccapane's father.

The man looked B.J. straight in the eye. He flushed with anger. Then, according to B.J., Ralph Ammaccapane leaned forward and said in a loud, menacing tone, "If you continue to lie about my daughter, I'll take your head off."

Shaken with fear, but also white hot with anger of his own, B.J. moved past the man and into the clubhouse. Michelle was completely stunned. "It was really upsetting," says Gilchrist, who tried to get between the two men. "Michelle's dad is everything to her. That hurt her a lot."

B.J. promptly sought out a USGA official and told him about the incident. He also requested additional security for his daughter. The official granted the request and assigned an extra guard to Michelle, bringing the detail to three in total, the number usually reserved for Tiger Woods. B.J. then handed her golf bag to Gilchrist.

Later that day, Michelle Wie shot a 73 for a two-day total of 146 (4 over) to become the youngest golfer ever to make the cut at the U.S. Women's Open. That was the real news, of course, but the press was still in a frenzy over the altercation that morning between B.J. Wie and Ralph Ammaccapane.

The weekend was without further incident, though certainly not without tension. The transition to Gilchrist worked smoothly, as Michelle made nearly all of the decisions on the course, something she'd been eager to do. To the surprise of even her biggest supporters, considering the circumstances, Wie played steady golf on Saturday and Sunday, shooting 76–76 to finish in the middle of the pack at 14 over.

Not too shabby for a 13-year-old.

But Michelle was still rattled by Thursday's unpleasant exchange with Danielle Ammaccapane and Friday's confrontation by her father. "Never," she told a reporter that Sunday night, "have I ever been so humiliated in all my life." She had come into the week full of confidence and enthusiasm, but she left Oregon with a strong dose of wariness. And so did her parents.

What had they learned from their first U.S. Open? The answers were telling.

B.J., ever the engineer: "I learned her swing must be more consistent."

Bo, ever the protective mother: "Don't talk to the media."

Michelle: "Sometimes a little snowball becomes a big snowball."

Skipping a Grade

No less an authority on golf than Tiger Woods weighed in on Michelle Wie at the start of 2004: "I think it's pretty neat that she's playing. But I also look at the philosophy, too. You need to play and win, too, learn the art of winning. My dad was a big believer in that. I didn't start playing nationally until I was playing well enough to win consistently at the junior level in my own Orange County."

B.J. and Michelle—or was it the other way around?—had already concluded that Michelle was done with junior golf.

But there were little signs. Like the dust-up with Danielle Ammaccapane (and then the golfer's father) at the 2003 U.S. Open. "Mentally, both Michelle and I were affected by the incident," B.J. told a reporter. "Her confidence was down. And her performance suffered. She struggled with her swing."

Later that year, B.J. and Bo noticed how happy Michelle

was to get away from golf and spend some time with her two cousins, Lynn and Jean, in Cerritos, California. They went to Knott's Berry Farm (ushered by an HBO crew). They stayed up until three o'clock in the morning every night, talking about everything besides golf. They laughed when strangers approached and asked, "Are you Michelle Wie?" Eventually, her parents began calling her "Andi" in public.

They watched movies constantly, from *How to Lose a Guy in 10 Days* to *The Hot Chick*. They watched Carson Daly and *Daria*. That Michelle had grown tired of all the travel was understandable: the family had left Hawaii in the spring, after school, and had spent the entire summer moving from town to town on the mainland. Michelle missed home, missed her friends, and missed her life. She didn't have e-mail—"My e-mail account expired!"—and she didn't own a cell phone. She missed her cousins. The Wies vowed to spend even more time with family in 2004.

That didn't happen.

There were little signs, like the way Michelle reacted to a jarring question at the 2004 U.S. Women's Open, at the Orchards in South Hadley, Massachusetts. Not the one from an American reporter about her double bogey on 16. Not another about her tricky punch from the poison ivy on 14. But the one from Michael Won, a reporter for the Los Angeles–based *Korea Daily*, who asked for Wie's reaction to the recent beheading by Islamic extremists in Iraq of a South Korean translator named Kim Sun Il.

Michelle froze. Her smile vanished. Her eyes widened in disbelief and sorrow.

"I felt sad," she started. "I don't know why they do this. . . ."

Then she collected herself and said, "I'm not really up on

politics. I'm a golfer, guys." It was a graceful recovery. But was she just a golfer? And if she was getting that type of query at 14, what would happen when she was older? What would happen when the kid gloves came off?

The little signs all pointed to the need to take it slower, to spend a bit more time getting used to this strange phase between adventure and business, between obscurity and fame. By now, B.J. and Bo knew that Michelle was going to be as special as they had always hoped. She had won only one tournament since spurning junior golf, but who wins an adult tournament at 13? In a sport where repeatability is precious, she performed the same perfect swing over and over again. When she lingered near the cut line of a tournament, she never looked for the safe option. She had guts.

So the little signs felt like just so many bumps in the road. Nothing to fret about. For Michelle Wie, the sky was still the limit. But there were big signs, too, and as 2004 began, they told a different story.

The roar was so loud at Honolulu's Waialae Country Club in January 2004 that it gave Garrett Kojima goose bumps.

The 36-year-old Realtor stood among more than a thousand people, drowning in a sound that he'd thought erupted only at University of Hawaii football games. He added to it, yelling for the local girl who had the courage to challenge the best male golfers in the world. Kojima had played a round with her only the year before, trying hard not to pop up his drive or shank an iron in front of her. Was this the same girl, charging up the back nine at the 2004 Sony Open with a chance to make a PGA cut?

"It was a feeling like she was playing a major," Kojima says. "Everyone roared. We never had that kind of excitement at the

Sony before. The whole state of Hawaii went Michelle Wie crazy."

The Sony Open, held every January in Honolulu, is the only PGA Tour stop on Oahu. (The other stop in Hawaii is the Mercedes-Benz Championship on Maui.) Wie tried to qualify on Monday in 2002 and 2003 but didn't make it. For 2004, Hawaii's governor, Linda Lingle, made a special request to the sponsors that they invite Wie to join the 143-player field. For Sony executives it was a no-brainer, what with all the publicity this 14-year-old phenom had been getting. "We wouldn't have invited a girl from New York or Florida," says Dale Nagata, Sony Hawaii general manager. "She was a special girl from Hawaii."

Good call: Wie's entry resulted in a 76 percent jump in attendance from 2003, just a sniff of the power of the idea of a teenage girl trying to compete against men.

But Wie was much more than an idea. That's what golf fans started to understand for the first time that week in 2004. Ernie Els requested a round with Wie and gave her a tip on how to chip out of deep rough. He also helped her slow her putting strokes. Craig Bowden, Wie's playing partner, told *Golf World,* "Give her five years. She'll be beating Annika."

But first she had to make the cut. Only the top 70 (and ties) would survive and play on the weekend. No woman had made a PGA Tour cut since 1945, when Babe Didrikson Zaharias did it at the Tucson Open. That feat, among many, earned Babe the title of "Greatest Female Athlete of the First Half of the 20th Century," given by the Associated Press. Wie making a PGA Tour cut at the tender age of 14 would put her on her way to earning the same distinction for the first half of the 21st century. A year earlier, Annika Sorenstam had played at the Colonial in Fort Worth and missed the cut by five strokes. Afterward she concluded she didn't belong on a men's tour.

Wie felt that she did.

"That whole entire fairway was lined with people, all the way down to the green," says family friend Tommy Kim. "She just hit it down the middle, walked off the tee, smiling like it was nothing. It didn't even faze her. Kevin Hayashi, her playing partner, saw me coming off the tee box. He was like, 'Man, my heart! Wanna play for me?' I think Michelle almost thrives on it."

Wie shot a 2-over 72 in the first round, making birdie on her third hole to put her name on the leaderboard for a brief time before consecutive bogeys. Three thousand people followed her around all day, many with pins that read "*Michelle No Ka Oi*" (Hawaiian for "Michelle is the best"). One golfer saw the mob, turned to his playing partners, and said, "I didn't know Tiger was here." Jesper Parnevik, admittedly relieved that he didn't get beaten by a 14-year-old girl, said that Wie's performance outdid Annika's by a hundredfold. Wie tied three former major champions—Shaun Micheel, Tom Lehman, and Jeff Sluman—and beat Tour mainstays Scott Hoch and Adam Scott. The round, and the scene, went beyond incredible all the way to surreal.

The AP's Doug Ferguson wrote that Wie would "probably" not play into the weekend, reasoning that she would have to shoot 67 to survive. No woman had ever shot that well in a men's event.

Friday brought an earthquake. Wie one-putted 12 of her final 14 greens, dropping two from more than 40 feet, in a last-ditch charge that left 5,000 spectators breathless as the sun set. Even veterans like Paul Azinger milled around the clubhouse asking how the girl was doing. Players stopped putting on the practice green when she played the nearby 9th hole. This wasn't a round of golf. This was an event. People wanted to witness a miracle.

Michelle came to the final three holes needing to play 3-under to make the cut. She stepped to the 16th tee without a single jitter and blasted a 311-yard drive, leaving a short approach shot that she dropped 15 feet behind the pin. She made that putt for birdie, her sixth of the tournament. On 17, Wie yanked her iron approach on a par 3 off the grandstand, but still got up and down to save par.

On the 18th, a 551-yard par 5, she needed an eagle. Wie scorched her drive 299 yards and nearly put her second shot on the green. But now she needed to hole out from the apron. She swung long and soft, and the gallery watched as her ball floated, landed below the hole, and rolled toward history.

It came up short.

So she didn't play into the weekend, but she had stretched imaginations all over the golf world. Michelle Wie *not* making the cut actually ranked as one of the biggest golf stories of the year.

But once again, her reaction was nearly as telling as the feat itself. She shot 68, and yet she didn't exult. "I can't believe it," she said indignantly. "I thought I just had to make birdie. And then I was like, 'Oh, no. This is *not* happening.' "

Fans felt the same way. They wanted more. An ESPN.com poll taken after the Sony Open found that nearly three-quarters of respondents wanted other PGA Tour sponsors to offer Wie an exemption. Even more stunning, more than 68 percent of those polled said Wie should go ahead and play more against the men. Seventy-two percent believed Wie would do for women's golf what Tiger Woods was doing for men's golf.

This 14-year-old girl had shot a 68 against men, and the golf world came unhinged. A Montreal man ripped out a Michelle Wie card from a sports collectors' magazine, put it on eBay, and sold it for $280. That card was one of more than four hundred Wie-related collectibles that appeared on the site in the days after Sony. The merely curious had suddenly become the addicted.

The problem with addictions, of course, is that the fix has to get greater and greater, and it's still not good enough.

Michelle had a new caddy at the Sony, a 38-year-old South African named Bobby Verwey.

Gary Gilchrist was six years old when he first met Verwey on a cricket pitch in South Africa. He took a cricket ball off the chin, and it was Verwey who rushed over to see if he was all right. The two became fast friends. Both had golf in their blood. Verwey was born into a line of top golfers—his father won three PGA Tour events, his grandfather the Senior British Open—and he was breaking par at age 11. He turned pro at nineteen. "I wasn't Michelle Wie," he says, "but I was bloody close."

Verwey never grew into the role his taskmaster father imagined for him. Still, he didn't stray from the game, and he went to Florida in 2000, where he ran into his old friend Gilchrist, who was working for golf guru David Leadbetter. Four years later, Gilchrist called him. By then, Verwey was caddying for his uncle, Gary Player. But Gilchrist needed a favor. Specifically, he needed a caddy. But not for himself.

"Come on," Verwey said when he heard whose bag Gilchrist was asking him to carry. "A 14-year-old girl trying to play on the PGA Tour?" It was true, Gilchrist insisted; he wasn't kidding. "Pay for my ticket," Verwey said, "and I'll fly out to Hawaii and see for myself." He did, and fell under Wie's spell as soon as he saw her golf swing: "It was the greatest thing I had ever seen. I can't put it into words. Perfection."

Verwey had seen a lot of golf over the years, but he was unprepared for this young girl who was almost oblivious to her potential. "Gary and I, both of us are Christians," Verwey says. "We saw her as a gift. It was as if she was an angel."

Gilchrist had devoted his professional life to young golfers. How many teachers wake up every morning hoping to come across one kid who has even a shot at a pro career? This kid was unlike any other, a once-in-a-lifetime talent, and Gilchrist had a chance to help her become one of the greatest golfers who ever lived.

Verwey gave himself three assignments that week in Hawaii: keep Michelle loose, help her gauge the wind, and help her read the greens. Other than that, he stood back and tried not to gawk when Wie outdrove Els on a hole during the practice round. On the greens, Verwey did give Wie his uncle Gary's number one tip on putting: hold your head still and focus on a single dimple on the ball, then keep watching that spot even after the putt starts rolling. During rounds, he commented on everything from the scenery to school to shopping, all to keep Michelle from getting nervous, and he encouraged her to shake off bad tee shots by focusing on her short game. Everything worked. Michelle had the best round, and the best putting day, of her entire life.

And still Gilchrist fretted. "B.J. is tough," he told Verwey. But the caddy shrugged it off. He had dealt with a hard-charging father all his life. "You leave B.J. to me," he told Gilchrist. But Verwey would later admit that he had never met a father as tough as this.

Even though he had commitments to Player, Verwey agreed to stay with Wie for two more tournaments. Together, and without consulting B.J., he and Gilchrist hatched a plan to give Michelle a few pointers at the first—the Safeway International in Phoenix—then "turn her loose" at the Kraft Nabisco Championship at the Mission Hills Country Club in Rancho

Mirage, California, the first of the four women's majors. That was the event, they promised themselves, that she would win.

In Arizona, a reporter asked Wie if she felt any different having Verwey on the bag instead of B.J. She joked that now she didn't have to fight with her dad for eighteen holes. Clever, and funny, but Verwey would look back on that moment as "the first sign of drama."

Michelle played well at Safeway until Sunday, when the winds picked up and the greens hardened. Gary Player always insisted that his caddy read putts for scoring instead of safety, so Verwey encouraged his young charge to be aggressive with her putter. He could tell later that night that B.J. was upset with his daughter's new style. The next morning, when Verwey asked if they could stop for coffee on the way to California, B.J. kept driving. The chill had set in.

When the group got to Rancho Mirage, B.J. approached Verwey on the practice green with what he called a "gravity machine." It was like a level, able to tell where the ground had no slope. The engineer in B.J. loved these types of gadgets, but Gilchrist was all about feel on greens. Verwey was the same; he tested greens simply by grabbing a handful of balls and rolling them.

B.J. started quizzing Verwey, asking him to find the spots on each green where there was no slope. *So I can caddy for Gary Player,* Verwey thought, *but I can't caddy for a 14-year-old girl?* Verwey went along with the exercise and guessed 12 slopes out of 12. Perfect score. What he wanted to tell B.J. was that reading greens has much more to do with intangibles than engineering. The grass is longer later in the day. There could be a bump from a prior hole placement, or a ball mark. Reading greens, he wanted to say, is not rocket science. But what he did tell B.J. was this: "If you want to caddy, here's the bag."

Bo and Michelle helped Verwey cool off, and told him to come back out in the afternoon. He did, and Michelle shot 3 under. And she did it with a brand-new driver. That was a cardinal sin, changing a club so close to a major. And during the first round on Thursday, Michelle brought out her own yardage book, scribbled with her father's notes. Verwey asked why. Michelle responded with no expression: "Because my dad told me to."

And so it went, all four rounds. Verwey might be on Michelle's bag, but B.J. was running the show. Only days before, she'd been treating Verwey like a trusted advisor, almost like an older brother. On Saturday, she went the whole day without speaking to Verwey at all. She made two club selections that caused the caddy to cringe, and wound up with two bogeys. *What's going on,* Verwey thought, *in this guy's head?* He knew, all too well, that the club choices had been B.J.'s.

Verwey had to love the results: 69, 72, and 69 on the first three rounds. She was only 14 years old! But the caddy, like so many Wie watchers in the years to come, believed she was capable of even better.

Wie got to the par-5 final hole just a few strokes off the lead. The tees were at the front, so Verwey pulled out her driver. "Michelle," he said, "you're two or three back. Bang it down there, make a three, and put some pressure on the players behind you." Any less club, he thought, would bring a fairway bunker into play. Wie looked at Verwey and said, "My dad told me to play safe and hit 5-wood here." Verwey slammed the driver back into the bag. Her tee shot found the bunker, and she had to scramble to save par. She finished fourth, four strokes behind winner Grace Park, who called Wie "awesome."

That would be the last hole Verwey ever caddied for Michelle Wie. He's wondered ever since if the "angel" would ever live up to her potential.

"That was the turning point in her career," he says, "right there."

What would she do for an encore? "We're not dumb," B.J. told *Golf World* in the immediate aftermath of the Sony coming-out party. "We will move with extreme caution. She's got some LPGA Tour events and a full USGA schedule. We're not going to jump into anything else right now."

The John Deere Classic called to offer a sponsor's exemption to the PGA Tour stop, and B.J. politely turned it down. The 84 Lumber Classic got the same answer. Ditto a *Vogue* magazine request for an interview and a photo spread. Then, in April, in an interview published in *ESPN The Magazine,* B.J. admitted to an oh-so-slight shift in his thinking:

> At first I thought there was no chance Michelle would turn professional before graduating from Stanford. But a second alternative is going to college and then choosing whether she will play for the men's team. The NCAA doesn't prohibit that. Or she could play for the girls' college team. Or she goes to a college, like Stanford, and not play on the golf team.

Yet the conservative side of his personality still shone through: "If she plays for money, she might not enjoy it. Now she doesn't have to worry about making money. She likes the carefree life. There's a big difference between college and high school. Turning pro in high school may not be a good idea."

Yet the stakes were growing, and B.J. knew it. As an amateur, his daughter walked away from each tournament with only a big smile from the event's sponsors, leaving behind what would have been a lot of big paychecks—more than $100,000 in the first half of 2004 alone. Yet her family had to front the funds for plane tickets, rental vans, food, and hotels. Their 2001 travel bill was in the neighborhood of $50,000. The following year, that figure rose to $70,000. And then $100,000. And then . . .

The bottom line: the cost of her not turning pro was becoming unbearable. The little signs may have shown a need to go slow, but the dollar signs screamed for speeding up.

"She should command more than any woman has ever made on the LPGA Tour," said one top agent that summer of 2004. "Endorsements could bank her $15–$20 million a year in her early years with the potential increasing as she proves herself."

"It's fun to read about endorsement deals," B.J. responded when he heard those figures bandied about. "But none of it's real."

So when would Michelle turn pro?

"October 11, 2007," became B.J.'s stock answer. "That's the earliest. Her 18th birthday."

Soon after Michelle's fourth-place finish in the Kraft Nabisco in March 2004, Gilchrist got a call from his boss, David Leadbetter. "When are you bringing her to me?" Leadbetter asked. Gilchrist knew what that meant: "I knew then and there that I'd be gone, that he was going to take over," Gilchrist says. "Deep down, I hoped he would support me. But I knew that wasn't in the cards. I knew he'd sell himself to the Wies."

In May, Leadbetter met up with the Wies at the Michelob ULTRA Open in Virginia. There, B.J. took Gilchrist aside for a talk while Leadbetter worked with Michelle on the range. "He said to me, 'I don't want you anywhere around while David's working with her,'" Gilchrist recalls. "He was very firm."

Gilchrist had never tinkered with Michelle's swing. He preferred to work on mental strength, course management, and overall "feel." Leadbetter's approach could not have been more different. He loved to isolate and analyze every component of the golf swing, like a biologist breaking a cell into its component parts. The Wies, scientists and perfectionists at heart, loved it. "He fed the parents' interest in the total golf game," Gilchrist said. "They were in awe."

B.J. then scheduled an appointment with sports psychologist Jim Loehr, author of the *New York Times* bestseller *The Power of Full Engagement,* which had received a full hour of discussion on *Oprah.* Loehr's clients included Monica Seles, Dan Jansen, Jim Courier, Mark O'Meara, Ray Mancini, and Eric Lindros. This was the big time.

Michelle Wie met Loehr at his office at the Human Performance Institute, a nine-acre campus ten minutes from the Orlando airport. Loehr usually starts a consultation by asking an athlete his or her goal. That's how he began with Wie. "Why," he asked, "does golf mean so much to you?"

"I guess I play golf," Wie said, "because I want to be a living testimony. Most barriers to women are self-imposed."

Loehr was stunned. "I about fell out of my chair," he said later. He asked Wie, "Where did you get that?"

Wie recoiled. She didn't like the suggestion that she was parroting someone else's words.

"All I've done is break records," she replied. "I started out on a boys' baseball team. I was the best hitter. Limitations are pretty artificial. I can be a statement for that."

Was she reciting from a script her parents had written? At the very least, Loehr thought, this was no dumb jock. "Emotionally and mentally, she learns very fast," Loehr told a reporter later. "She has an extraordinary ability to listen and absorb. Her optimism and her resiliency are amazing. She is a gentle soul who is able to see beyond herself."

Most people assume that a sports psychologist's only goal is to help athletes take full advantage of their gifts. Loehr wasn't as worried about that as he was about making sure Michelle's gifts didn't take advantage of her: "I'm more concerned about golf's effect on her than what she'll achieve when the journey is over. The things that would typically scare people to death aren't a big barrier for her. She wants to make sure she doesn't let people down, that she doesn't fizzle out."

Loehr began a relationship with Wie that included regular telephone conversations, and not just about golf. Loehr helped Wie think optimistically about her one academic phobia: math tests. That was an odd barrier for a girl from such a gifted mathematical family, but Loehr helped Wie calm down, and her test scores responded.

The Wies marveled at Loehr's impact, but the therapist worried about the future. Wie had started down a very original path in one sense, but one that was all too familiar to Loehr. Here's what he said at the time:

> I see her as this very innocent, wonderful young girl, going into a world of pro sport that is brutal. How does she fly commercial? Live in a community that's not gated? I hope that with all this praise and glory and attention, she stays grounded to the most important realities in her life. I hope we can create a structure to allow her to grow. This is not going to go down without lots and lots of difficult times.

Difficult times? Nowhere in sight.

In June 2004, Wie traveled to England to play in the Curtis Cup, the youngest competitor ever to do so. She won two singles matches for the U.S. team in front of an adoring crowd at Formby Golf Club in Merseyside, each time running back after she'd finished to cheer her teammates to victory.

The next month, she became only the second amateur to get an exemption to the U.S. Women's Open. The debate about the decision took up most of the buzz and the pre-tournament press conference. The USGA reasoned she would have finished 28th on the 2003 LPGA Tour money list had she not been an amateur, and the top 35 earners get passes to the Open. But to some critics that seemed like a fabricated excuse rather than a reason. Simply by being different and marketable, critics wailed, Wie was getting special treatment from the USGA.

"Just because she is a special young player is no reason she should get special treatment," wrote *Golf World*'s Ron Sirak. "Furthermore, it is not a reason the rules and spirit of the game should be violated. Let's reward achievement, not potential."

But grumbling quieted when Wie finished 13th with a stunning 1-over 71–70–71–73. That earned her a return trip to the Open the following year at Cherry Hills, just outside Denver.

All told, Wie had to walk away from more than a quarter of a million dollars after her seven LPGA Tour events in 2004. She didn't miss a cut. She was amazing, consistent, and consistently amazing.

Little signs? Sure. But you had to look really hard for them. Wie would not be playing junior or amateur tournaments anymore.

For better or for worse, she had skipped ahead.

6

The Manifesto

The Wies, normally impervious (or at least unrespon-
sive) to criticism, decided to respond to those who believed Michelle was moving too far too fast. They
made their case in an open letter that Michelle (or, quite possibly, her father) wrote and sent to Doug Ferguson of the Associated Press. Here is a slightly condensed version:

> *I would like to take this opportunity to clarify myself with re-*
> *gards to . . . not following the conventional path that many*
> *great golfers have gone through.*
>
> *I wanted to play in the AJGA national junior golf tour-*
> *naments, but I wasn't allowed to play. I was too young.*
>
> *By the time I was allowed to play in the AJGA tourna-*
> *ments at age 13, I already made in the top 10 at a LPGA*
> *major and won an adult USGA amateur tournament. I had*
> *the choice of concentrating only on junior tournaments or*

playing the combination of professional and USGA tournaments. I chose the latter.

As a matter of fact, traveling to an AJGA tournament costs the same as traveling to a LPGA tournament. If Bentley and Toyota cost the same, wouldn't anyone get a Bentley? I got a Bentley and I do not regret my decision.

People always ask why I do . . . not just follow the conventional path. My answer is very simple. I always wanted to push myself to the limit. I started walking when I was 9 months old and I started reading when I was just over one year old. I started playing golf when I was 4 and shot a 64 when I was 10. . . . I always wanted to do things fast. I always wanted to be the first and youngest to do things.

I feel grateful for all the sponsor exemptions that the tournaments have offered to me. . . . This is my fourth year playing on the LPGA Tour. I now feel comfortable with the players and the Tour itself. When I first came out on the tour, I felt lost and confused. . . . But as I played more events, the Tour felt more and more like home.

A lot of people criticize my choice to play in the PGA Tour events, but . . . it's really fun and I think it helps me to get ready for my ultimate goal of becoming a PGA Tour member.

I am not afraid of failure, and I cannot be. When I went to the Great Wall of China, I was really excited. I was walking up the stairs and going really high. I got tired and I looked down. At that point I saw how high I was and I saw what would happen if I fell. I collapsed right at that very moment and sat down on the steps. I refused to go another step higher and crawled my way down. I feel that if I get afraid of failure, then I can't go any higher. Now I regret that I did not walk up higher to see what is up there.

A lot of the critics say that . . . missing cuts in PGA events will ruin my confidence. I don't believe in that statement. . . . When I go out and play in a PGA Tour event, I don't go there to win now, but to learn from the best.

No matter what the critics say about me, I am going to do whatever my heart tells me to do, and I thank my parents for always backing me up. Dream big and I will reach the sky; dream small and my feet will never get off the ground.

Thanks,

Michelle Wie

Almost immediately, the letter came to be known as "the Manifesto."

The question of authorship aside, the Manifesto reveals much about the family's state of mind at that crucial time.

The point about junior golf is correct: Michelle couldn't have joined the AJGA even if she wanted to when she was 10 and already making golf news. But the Manifesto doesn't explain why she didn't play junior tournaments against Morgan Pressel, Paula Creamer, and some of the South Koreans who would soon announce themselves as the heiresses to Se Ri Pak's legacy.

Did she think she had nothing to learn from them? Apparently so: she compared the AJGA to a Toyota versus her ride of choice, a Bentley. That one line, by the way, became a lightning rod for Wie critics, who lambasted her for behaving as if she were entitled, for wanting to bypass all the hurdles her peers had to clear. Wasn't she too young to drive a car anyway?

The Great Wall of China story was revealing, though perhaps not in the way she (and/or B.J.) intended. Wie's talent had boosted her very high very fast. Her decision to skip junior golf only made the air thinner. The more she climbed, the scarier it would be to look down.

"She has set goals so high that only one person will achieve them," said LPGA veteran and friend Christina Kim. "I pray that she will. Otherwise it's a damn long way to fall."

The frenzy bubbled to such a pitch that McDonald's, the sponsor of the 2005 LPGA Championship, threatened to pull its affiliation if Wie was not allowed to enter the major. The LPGA caved, and Wie became the first-ever amateur to play in that event.

Many female golfers were incredulous at the hype and angered by the special treatment—how could a nonmember be allowed to play for the LPGA title?—yet Wie temporarily silenced the critics again by finishing second, three strokes behind winner Annika Sorenstam. She was the only player in the field to shoot all four rounds under par. The $140,000 she couldn't accept because of her amateur status boosted her 2005 season "earnings" to more than $300,000. Her inability to cash the check for second meant an extra $36,000 to each of the two players tied for third, Laura Davies and—wouldn't you know it?—Paula Creamer.

"Good for them," Wie said. "They better give me some of that." And then: "Just kidding. I don't really care about that stuff."

But that summer, the pressure Wie seemed to enjoy—or at least brush off—finally seemed to creep up on her. She entered the final round of the 2005 U.S. Women's Open in Denver in a tie for the lead after rounds of 69–73–72. The Open won its highest Sunday TV rating in eight years, in large part because fans wanted to see Wie's best shot at golf's most important women's tournament.

The day was a total nightmare from the first hole, which Wie double-bogeyed. She then bogeyed the 3rd, 4th, and 8th holes before doubling the 9th for a 42—7 strokes over par. The back nine was almost as bad: 40. The 82 (only one golfer posted a worse score on that day) dropped her to 12 over for the tournament, 9 strokes behind winner Birdie Kim, and all the way into an eight-way tie for 23rd.

The most troubling sight for Wie fans was her putting. She missed three putts from inside 4 feet, often blinking back tears as she watched her ball avoid the hole. She half joked about her day in the press tent afterward, saying she needed a GPS device to find her ball, but the performance was nothing short of a collapse. It was the first time Wie had started a final round of a golf tournament under so much pressure, and it's a considerable understatement to say that she didn't perform with her usual calm.

Not even close.

And still . . .

A few days later at the PGA Tour's John Deere Classic in Silvis, Illinois, she came back strong, as if the U.S. Open collapse had never happened, and shot 2 under on Thursday. The next day, she commanded by far the biggest galleries of the day as Wie-watchers turned out to see if she could make history by making the cut. The John Deere's characteristic carnival atmosphere—tractor pulls, clowns, games for kids, even a "freak show"—only grew as Wie entered the last four holes at 4 under, one shot ahead of the projected cut line. But once again, as if the moment suddenly got too heavy for her to bear, she pulled her 3-wood into a bunker, found another bunker with her next shot, then three-putted for a double bogey.

So twice in three weeks, Michelle Wie played herself to the

verge of making history only to fall short at the last moment. But how could anyone criticize a 15-year-old girl for coming down with a case of the nerves in either situation? That's what golf is all about.

"I think it's very difficult to put into perspective what Michelle Wie is doing," said Phil Mickelson at the time. "I would be amazed if this was a 15-year-old boy playing in men's tournaments and coming within a few strokes of making the cut in a PGA Tour event. When I was 17, I couldn't come close to making a cut. I just can't believe any 15-year-old, especially a girl, could be doing what she's doing. I can't fathom it."

Greg Norman seconded that emotion: "Golf has seen some phenomenal changes in the last 30 years, but Michelle Wie? I so wanted her to do it, it would have been great. But it's only a matter of time."

The youngest male ever to make a PGA cut, by the way, was Bob Panasik, who did the trick in 1957 at the Bell Canadian Open. He was 15 years, 8 months, and 20 days old—almost exactly Wie's age at the time she came oh-so-close at the John Deere.

But making a PGA cut was nothing compared to what Wie tried to do next.

Greg Johnston grew up without golf in his blood or in his mind. He stumbled into it in the summer of 1987, when he signed up to be a caddy at the Corning Classic in his hometown, Corning, New York, to make a few bucks. One thing led to another, and seven years later he was on the bag of one of the LPGA's most popular players, Juli Inkster.

Then, in 2003, Inkster had to pull out of a Portland tournament at the last minute, and Johnston got a call from B.J.

Wie. His daughter needed a caddy for the Safeway Classic. Could he fill in just for the week? Johnston said sure, why not? Inkster didn't mind at all. She advised him to keep in touch with the Wies after the tournament, because she wouldn't play forever, and she wanted her friend to have a place to go after she left the scene.

Just before the first round of the tournament, B.J. steered his daughter aside and said, with Johnston standing next to them, "Michelle, you do everything Greg says."

That would stick with Johnston for a long time.

Wie followed Johnston's lead on the odd occasion when he filled in again over the next two years. He had never seen any girl swing so well or hit so far. He had no idea how to advise her at first, since she hit mid-irons where some women players hit woods. So he simply read her putts and watched her go. Wie finished 6th in the 2004 Wendy's Championship in Ohio, after which she and her family drove to a Cincinnati suburb for the U.S. Amateur Public Links championship, the male equivalent of the only tournament Wie won. Except there were two huge differences: a woman had never entered this event, and the winner got an invitation to the Masters.

Johnston booked a flight to Europe on the same day as the Sunday final, figuring he'd leave after Wie was eliminated, return home to Virginia, and fly to meet Inkster for the Evian Masters. The only risk to his travel plans was if Wie made the final. It was not a huge chance to take, Johnston figured, since no woman had ever even made it out of stroke play in the qualifying stage of any USGA men's event, let alone reached the end of the 64-player match play bracket. Even B.J. had booked his family's ticket to Europe for the Evian Masters in advance.

Then Wie made it through stroke play, shooting 76 and 72

to make the round of 64 by one stroke. And Johnston started thinking about that plane ticket.

Wie's first-round opponent was Will Claxton, a strong college player from Auburn. Not much of a matchup: a 15-year-old girl against a dominant college male. But somehow Wie came from two holes down to tie the match going into the final hole, a 420-yard par 4 that ended in a peninsula green.

After her drive, she had 180 yards to the pin, which was tucked left and precariously near the pond. Johnston, once again, didn't quite know what club to suggest. It didn't matter. Wie silently took out a 6-iron and aimed for the flag. It was the first of many times when Johnston wondered to himself how the girl thought she could make such a shot. But he stood back and watched the ball arc right at the pin and drop onto the green like a feather, 15 feet from the hole. Wie sank the birdie putt and won the match.

"She's a great golfer," Claxton said afterward. "But I guess you already know that. The whole world knows that."

The next day, a knot of USGA officials gathered behind the first tee to observe how opponents reacted to Wie. One college-age boy actually seemed to shake in his spikes, terrified of losing to a 15-year-old girl; Wie creamed him. An older gentleman got so rattled that he asked his caddy to fetch him a beer between the 9th green and the 10th hole; Wie dispatched him before he could finish his beverage.

She was the only person on the course not surprised by her success.

Wie beat three opponents and made the quarterfinals, going the improbable distance from one girl against 63 men to one girl against seven. Johnston now had two different bags to carry on two different continents. Additional ropes were brought in from the U.S. Senior Open in nearby Kettering just to keep the crowds contained. Journalists from *The New York Times, Sports Illustrated,* ESPN, and the Golf Channel hurried to Cincinnati, so many that USGA officials ran out of press passes and reporters had to write their names on labels and stick them on their shirts.

At St. Andrews, reporters gathered at the British Open to witness Jack Nicklaus' last trip across Swilcan Bridge started to huddle around computer screens in the media tent. Someone would scream out Wie's score after each hole, causing the tent to fill with an excited buzz.

Michelle Wie stood 36 hours and three rounds of golf away from qualifying for the Masters, the most prestigious golf event at the most exclusive golf club in America, one that did not allow women to become members.

Clay Ogden laughed when he first saw the mob around Wie as he made his way to the first tee in the quarterfinals on that sticky July Friday morning. "I was like, 'What is this?' " he recalled. Ogden was only 20 and a rising sophomore at Brigham Young University, but he had power and cool and looked almost ready to step out onto the PGA Tour. And he loved playing for big crowds.

But to Ogden, a big crowd was 75 people. Now he had to play in front of thousands. "There were people lined up three deep around the tee box," Ogden said. "And 75 yards down the fairway. It was crazy."

It was a day Ogden never forgot. "I remember everything," he said a year later. He remembered the way Wie struck the ball, the way she whipped through her turn without losing any balance, the way she handled the pressure as if it was nothing.

He even remembered specific shots, like on the 4th when Wie nailed a 190-yard approach to within 15 feet of the hole. Ogden took out his 5-iron and stared at the white speck right by the pin. He had no choice but to aim for Wie's ball. He did, and watched as his shot sailed right at it, then landed even closer to the flag. Ogden birdied four of his first five holes. ("I was in a zone.")

Ogden noticed something else: "I would say 'Good shot' or 'Good putt,' but I never got any response out of her." He wondered why. Was Wie simply in her own world? Didn't she know anything about common golf etiquette? Was she just plain rude? Or was it something else? "If somebody gives you a compliment," he said, "respond to it. At least acknowledge it."

But people in the gallery didn't know or care. When Ogden made a good shot, which was often on this day, one single man was heard applauding or cheering above the mostly silent gallery: Ogden's father. But even as his son birdied hole after hole, the chatter remained about the girl:

Beyond comprehension . . .

So much more confident than most boys . . .

I wish I could play like a 15-year-old girl . . .

But on this day, Ogden was better. And in the shadows of the tree-lined 14th green, he went up 5 to 4 and eliminated the 15-year-old from Hawaii. The crowd erupted in applause, as much for the girl's valiant effort as for the boy's victory. No one in the gallery knew it at the time, but the match that day was the last time Michelle Wie would ever play a tournament in the United States as an amateur.

Later that night, USGA official Marty Parkes checked into his hotel and logged on to check Google's top news stories for the day. Leading the pack was Karl Rove testifying in front of a grand jury. Next was a story on the aftermath of the London subway bombings. The third biggest story of the day (per

Google) was Michelle Wie falling just short in her quest to qualify for the Masters.

The days ahead would bring what can only be called "Michelle mania." Example: a Seattle newspaper column with the headline "Wie Wins 2015 Masters," in which the columnist called the missed cut "a trifle, a necessary plot turn for what will become a great—and historic—American success story."

Only an hour or so after the match with Ogden, Michelle gabbed animatedly on her cell phone as her parents loaded up their rented minivan. The three Wies jumped into the van and rode to a nearby Italian restaurant. Michelle wanted to order quickly so she could see a showing of *Charlie and the Chocolate Factory* starring her favorite actor, Johnny Depp.

She was a kid again.

The three settled in at a circular table. Bread came, and B.J. dived in, but Michelle simply watched, saying she was on a diet. B.J. talked about the family's upcoming trip to Europe for two tournaments and a fashion show featuring his daughter, followed by a return to New York for an appearance on *Late Show with David Letterman*. The Wies grinned as the waiter went through his list of specials.

But then the subject of the weekend's tournament came up again, and the mood at the table shifted. "I don't feel like I've proven anything yet," Michelle said. And she told a story about the men's tournament on Oahu she'd tried to enter as a child. "They said, 'Men only. Always has been, always will be,'" Wie remembered with a set jaw and no smile. "I never got to play that tournament."

B.J. chimed in: "Most of the criticisms of her are unreasonable. They are encouraging a very small dream. That bothers me."

"It's the *P*GA Tour," Michelle said emphatically. "Not the *M*PGA. I don't think it's insulting or degrading anyone by stating my goals. I have different ways of doing things. I don't want to be seen as a woman golfer breaking barriers. I want to make people think."

But she had already done that earlier that same day. Now the name Michelle Wie meant "The Girl Who Plays Against Men." She had come so far so fast that the only thing left to prove was that she could actually win on the LPGA Tour and actually compete on the PGA Tour. Suddenly the world wanted that to happen fast. And perhaps more importantly, the Wies themselves wanted it to happen fast. So B.J. called Johnston soon after the U.S. Publinx and told him that Michelle was turning pro, and that the family wanted him as their full-time caddy.

Juli Inkster had figured she would lose Johnston sooner or later, maybe in three years or so, but it happened much, much sooner than either expected. She was upset. Johnston was torn. But the decision was as obvious to the caddy as it was to the family.

The time was now.

7

Wie, Inc.

On October 5, 2005, the Wies woke up early, drove five miles south toward the sea, and checked into a suite at the Kahala Mandarin Oriental hotel, right next door to the Waialae Country Club where Michelle had burst onto the national scene with her 68 at the Sony Open the year before. The Wies took a wood-paneled elevator up to their suite, which normally goes for $1,800 to $2,000 a night and has a balcony overlooking the Pacific complete with a pair of black binoculars for watching sailboats and sunbathers. As Janice, her longtime beautician, styled her hair in the bathroom, Michelle looked herself over in the mirror and beamed.

Downstairs in the hotel, outside the Maile Ballroom, B.J. greeted friends and family with big handshakes and a toothy grin as they made their way inside, where a small army of photographers and videographers and reporters was already set up. To B.J., the hoopla felt like a wedding, albeit something of a shotgun ceremony, since the event had been put together in only three days.

Running the show for the Wies was Ken Sunshine Consultants, a self-described "boutique public relations and communications consulting firm" that represented stars such as Jon Bon Jovi, Leonardo DiCaprio, and Barbra Streisand. Point man Jesse Derris, a 25-year-old Wisconsin graduate, had served in 2004 as spokesman for John Kerry and Howard Dean, so for him the day's events had the headlong rush of a campaign advance. Derris seemed right at home, even though he had misspelled *Wie* on the press release.

Michelle, typically, showed no sign of worry or concern. Like any bride, she felt the day was meant to be. Today, six days shy of her sixteenth birthday, she would turn professional.

There was no apparent reason why Michelle couldn't handle the transition from amateur to professional with her usual aplomb. Her days were already loaded. She got to school by 7:30 each morning, and left at 2:30 for two and a half hours of golf. On Tuesdays, she went to a spa for a massage, a mani-pedi, and then maybe some shopping at the Ala Moana outdoor mall. Every Saturday and Sunday, she spent six hours at the course, and went out with friends to the mall or a movie in the evenings. She had five close friends from the elite Punahou School, all overachievers, like her.

Yet even with the manic schedule and enough pressure to stagger your average adult, Michelle never disappointed anyone, whether autograph-seeking fans, story-seeking journalists, or grade-seeking teachers. She never seemed to crack.

This day would be no exception.

Up on the dais with her was a new member of the family.

He had an easy smile, but he seemed a lot more anxious than the teenager with him. When he took the microphone, sitting in a director's chair, he mistakenly announced that Michelle's new priorities would be golf and then school. He caught himself, laughed, and then apologized to B.J. and Bo, who also laughed. Then he turned to Michelle, blushing slightly, and said, "No, I'm not nervous."

Ross Berlin could be forgiven. He was one of many newcomers swept into the orbit of Planet Wie. An attorney by trade, educated at Wake Forest and then at Michigan State, he had joined a law firm in California, where he had quickly gravitated toward sports. While overseeing venue selection for the 1994 World Cup, Berlin learned to master the mix of sports and entertainment. He jumped from soccer to golf and continued working in stadium and arena development, always focusing on what fans wanted and athletes needed. In 1999, he joined the PGA Tour as a vice president of sales and marketing, with responsibility for cultivating and cementing relationships with title sponsors.

For a people person, a guy with a kind word and a handshake for everyone, it was a natural fit. Then, in the summer of 2005, he got a call from the William Morris Agency. When Dave Wirtschafter, the president of the agency, bid him hello from the agency's office in Beverly Hills, Berlin wondered if this was some sort of mistake. It wasn't.

William Morris wasn't known for managing athletes. Morris was the legendary home of megastars like Clark Gable, Will Rogers, and Judy Garland. Athletes, particularly golfers, usually wound up at IMG, where Arnold Palmer and Mark McCormick had teamed up in the 1960s and revolutionized sports representation. True, Venus and Serena Williams signed up with William Morris, but they were looking beyond tennis to fashion and entertainment. In fact, it was their crossover appeal that convinced the agency to broaden its scope. So of all the surprises Berlin stumbled upon during that phone call, the least was when Wirtschafter told him his agency had a shot at representing Michelle Wie.

It made sense. The line between sports and entertainment had blurred over the course of Michelle's life. When she was born in 1989, a man on the street in L.A. with a number 32 jersey was equal parts Lakers fan and Magic Johnson fan. Then Michael Jordan changed that.

The progenitor of a new breed of sports hero, MJ did not seem out of place in a boardroom, on a men's magazine cover, or in a commercial. He could do it all. Even fans of opposing teams wanted to "Be Like Mike." He was as much a personality as a team player, and so he became his own brand. He spurred Nike's eclipse of Converse with a five-year deal that included his own line of shoes, a perk no other NBA star could claim. The investment paid off: the Air Jordan shoe made $100 million in 1985 alone. Deals ensued with corporations from Coca-Cola to McDonald's to Chevrolet.

Jordan's agent, David Falk, spoke openly about how stars like Jordan "should be paid a disproportionate amount of money." To Falk, the athlete was above the team, at least in marketability, and that idea quickly took hold throughout the sports world. In one six-day span in 1996, the agent negotiated $335 million in deals for six of his NBA clients.

Sports and entertainment became inseparable.

When Jordan left basketball in the late 1990s, the sports world ached for a replacement—the Next Jordan. At the same time, athletes became infinitely more knowable through cable TV and the Internet. Fans could become well acquainted with their heroes almost immediately, and they also could analyze their performances almost as soon as games ended.

The search for the next great athlete quickly morphed with

great expectations. Sports only happened during games. But entertainment could happen all the time, so why not blend the two? In a 24/7 media blitz, was there even a choice?

This is the world Michelle Wie grew up in. When she was three, there were only eight pages on this new thing called the World Wide Web. When she won her only major amateur tournament, 10 years later, most people learned of the achievement through the Web. Wie was the first major sports star to be raised in the Internet era, and the first to have no memory of a world without the Web.

"We live in a Page Six society," said Maxximum Marketing VP Gil Pagovich. "It's more important to have the iconic status generated by things outside the playing field. The media knows what sells papers. Television has changed, too. A lot of the long-standing shows don't exist in the American culture anymore. They've been replaced by people looking for fifteen minutes of fame."

A predictable side effect of the rush to exploit the shorter attention spans and the quicker news cycles is that controversy draws a bigger buzz than solid achievement. Athletes such as Tim Duncan, LaDainian Tomlinson, Roger Federer, and Annika Sorenstam are hugely successful, but they don't draw as many online clicks as do controversial superstars such as Terrell Owens, Alex Rodriguez, and Barry Bonds. The Internet has added new access to the antihero, and thus more avenues to stoke the resentment. The more a disgruntled fan knows, the more he finds to dislike, and the more he dislikes, the more he wants to know, and so the spiral goes.

But today's Page Six society also has an insatiable desire to know who and what are on the horizon, who and what are coming to create the new buzz.

Michelle Wie was a perfect storm, the ultimate in Next. She

was only six days shy of her 16th birthday. She spurred debate and resentment and discussion and plenty of prediction. She was all future, all potential, all entertainment, a thrill ride and a flash point. For sponsors, she could represent almost any demographic: youth, girls, women, sports fans, Americans, Asians. She was a brand in the making, especially in a high-class sport where ads for Rolex and Infiniti appeared more often than those for Tide and Busch.

William Morris took note that everyone wanted to watch her, even if she didn't win. For fans, she was constant watercooler material, especially among those who played golf regularly, who often had the most disposable income and the most time. So in a world craving for the future, she fit anyone's imagination of what the future should be.

B.J. Wie always felt his daughter was above and beyond the typical athlete. Michelle herself spoke of breaking barriers more than she spoke of winning. She wrote in the Manifesto that she wanted to be "the first and the youngest to do things." She envisioned a life for herself beyond golf, perhaps in the fashion or modeling industry. She studied Japanese and Chinese in school, she loved to travel, and she considered majoring in business in college.

Consumers could look to her as a leader in style as well as substance. She could build a shelf life not just for the next 10 years on the course, but for the next 50 or 60 years all over the planet. She wouldn't be like Arnold Palmer, who was known only as a great golfer. She wouldn't even be like Tiger Woods, who was known as the ultimate champion. Wie didn't fit completely into any one athletic mold, and so, it could be argued, agencies such as IMG and Octagon would have no idea what to do with her. There was simply no other athlete with so many realms to explore, so she and William Morris, an agency with a strong handle on stage and screen, were a perfect fit. Golf was only the tip of the iceberg, and what would IMG or Octagon do once she had conquered golf?

But B.J. also knew very well that his daughter was still a golfer, as least for the short term. He wanted a manager who knew the game, and he wasn't going to sign with William Morris until the agency found someone who could walk in both worlds. Enter Berlin.

Easygoing yet sharp, Berlin could get along with even the most hardened of reporters. He knew the men's game—crucial for Wie's future—and he wouldn't be cowed by negotiations with global companies. Berlin had little experience as an agent, but that didn't matter when he waltzed into a New York hotel room to make his presentation to B.J. and Bo about how to capitalize on such rare potential. Berlin knew how to take advantage of every aspect of sports business, from marketing to advertising to law to media. He wasn't the typical agent, or even the typical lawyer. There didn't seem to be an ounce of fakery about him. B.J. and Bo and Michelle all liked Berlin immediately.

William Morris had picked the right man.

The hard part was managing the astronomical expectations.

"The most valuable attribute is yet-to-be-realized potential," said Peter Carlisle of Octagon, who ushered swimmer Michael Phelps from a 15-year-old unknown into a 23-year-old marketing megastar. "The double-edge sword is expectations raised in the media."

For Wie, expectations could not have been higher. She was destined, in the minds of many fans and journalists and even herself, to cause a seismic reaction. Even if she became the best female golfer on the planet, that still might not be enough, since she spoke about playing in the Masters.

"I made my goals very high," she explained at the time all this was going on. "It's going to be very hard for me to make a men's cut. I have to practice really hard. No one has ever done it before. But I enjoy that."

The Wies seemed to relish the attention, the pressure, the buzz. Their worst fear, it seemed, was no attention at all. After the men's Public Links tournament, B.J. said that skeptics "are encouraging a very small dream, and that bothers me." Michelle herself even defended those in the media who gossiped about her. "Critics are there for a reason," she said. "To point out things. Everyone has his or her own points of view. Everything isn't going to be all good or all bad."

Usually, agents and public relations experts come in to manage expectations. "If you were to develop a corporate partnership," Carlisle says, "I'd say, 'Let's not talk about the next big thing. Let's make sure we control all of that.' You'd wait for her to deliver and then market against that. In golf, the longevity is insane. For a younger athlete, my strategy might be much more conservative. You can defuse expectations and keep things quieter."

The Wies did not think that way.

"Youth goes really fast," said B.J. "She'll be 16. She's getting old."

Paula Creamer, an LPGA rookie at 18, won two tournaments in 2005 and became a budding starlet in her own right. Morgan Pressel joined the Tour in 2006, five months before her 18th birthday, and the next year won the Kraft Nabisco, making her the youngest player in LPGA history to win a major. The window in which Michelle could set a new mark was very tiny.

Was there room enough for more than one teenage darling in women's golf?

Michelle opened the proceedings in the Maile Ballroom by announcing that she was pledging $500,000 to the Hurricane Katrina relief effort. A little later, she fielded questions from the reporters there in Honolulu as well as those at satellite locations. One asked her to name the biggest pro and the biggest con about turning pro. She couldn't name a single con.

The Wies went to a friend's house for dinner and then watched the media coverage of the announcement that day. Michelle paid little attention to the television. She played with her new Sony Vaio phone, gabbing with friends about what had happened at school.

Few questioned the decision to turn pro. After all, millions of dollars in endorsements—serious money—would be hers for the signing of a contract once she was a professional, and a major injury as an amateur would put a huge payday like that at risk. Going pro was a no-brainer.

But what were her goals? To play in the Masters? To dominate the LPGA Tour? To break barriers, shatter stereotypes, create a whole new paradigm in sports?

None of those really fit neatly together. If playing in the Masters were her number one priority, she could have waited another year and tried another attempt at the U.S. Amateur Public Links. Now, as a pro, that way in was out. If she wanted to dominate the LPGA Tour by age 20, as her father had recently stated was her number one goal, she would have to focus on that—go to Q-School, get her card, and become a full-fledged member of the LPGA. But that went against her desire to "make people think" by competing against men. "That's what motivates me," she said. "How I might influence other people's lives, how I might make an impact on the world."

Her goal, it seemed, was to do everything, and to do it as quickly as possible. And that tall order was to be accomplished by a teenage girl who was still a full-time student and had no idea of the stresses and complexities of the fishbowl world she was about to enter, with only her equally unprepared parents and a rookie agent to guide her.

"If there was ever a golfer who should have gone down the center of the fairway, it would be her," *Golf World* columnist John Hawkins said after Wie's signing. "Go with IMG or Octagon and let the thing unfold instead of going with William Morris, which has no golf experience. I wouldn't have signed with a Hollywood star bureau. I just wonder what her priorities are. To be famous? Or a great golfer? Fame is such a cheap, low bar. At some point fame seemed to become more important than greatness. I think she's a little afraid. I think she's gotten some bad advice."

The choice of William Morris made a statement: the Wies' goal was to do *everything*—all of the above. Choosing IMG or Octagon would have provided a safety net, or at least guardrails. Choosing William Morris fit with the absolute best-case scenario. If Michelle could do anything and everything without a stumble, William Morris was the right agency.

B.J. Wie had prepared his daughter for unqualified success, without protecting her from possible failure.

The Samsung World Championship at the Bighorn Golf Club in Palm Desert provided the perfect launching pad for Michelle's pro career. Scheduled to begin two days after her 16th birthday, the tournament featured only 20 players, and it had no cut, a sizeable purse, and NBC cameras. That area of California had always been kind to Michelle's game. Also, it didn't hurt that a major South Korean company was the tournament sponsor. Or that the Wies wanted to buy a house on course property. Or that *Fortune* magazine wanted to put Michelle on its October cover to announce that Wie, Inc. was open for business.

"The reason for turning pro a few days early is to have the option of making the week of Samsung," B.J. told a reporter. "She'll do homework in advance, and take some with her." He said the family would not go out to dinner on October 11, the actual night of Michelle's 16th birthday. (Michelle was deluged by cakes anyway.)

For everything to fall into place, Berlin would have to move a mountain: finalize at least two multimillion-dollar deals with major international corporations in less than a month, all while doing his day job with the PGA Tour during the height of the golf season. And if he failed to seal the deals or (worse still) if William Morris lost the Wie account to IMG or Octagon—both of which showed interest—all his work would be for nothing.

If William Morris had no Wie account, what place did it have for someone like him?

The first big deal Berlin brought to the table was with Nike, with whom the Wies had enjoyed a relationship since Greg Nared reached out to B.J. a year earlier. A tall, athletic man with a soft voice, Nared had walked the ropes for years as Nike's on-site rep for Tiger Woods. Michelle had modeled Titleist and Adidas gear—occasionally at the same time, almost as if to tease her various suitors—but she loved the Nike drivers, Nike balls, Nike apparel, and, naturally, the Nike affiliation with Tiger.

Most important of all, Nike could put Wie in clothing that made a statement. She was entering a buttoned-down world where few athletes were fashion mavericks, but she had no intention of putting on a golf cap, collared shirt, and skirt and leaving it at that. She wanted to wear bucket hats and bright-colored shirts and loud belt buckles and chandelier earrings and maybe even cowboy boots. When she played against the men, she would make golf pants look comfortable and feminine. Wie could usher in an entirely new era for Nike, and vice versa.

Berlin then wrapped up a deal with Sony, which made equal sense for completely different reasons. Michelle was huge in Japan and South Korea, as was Sony. Sony also gave Michelle a technological platform that Nike could not. Instant messaging, texting, and camera phones were SOP to her, not foreign or frightening. She was just entering a demographic that not only craved the newest gadgets but actually needed them to survive in an online world. What Sony device would not look good in her oversized hands or in her purse as she hopped from country to country?

The Nike-Sony pairing was perfect, and Berlin negotiated a reported $10 million per year for five years that made Michelle the highest-paid female athlete in the world behind tennis icons Maria Sharapova and Serena Williams. With golf's longevity and fan demographic, Wie had the potential to become the highest-paid female athlete ever. And that projection didn't take into account the rapidly growing Asian markets, including China. Berlin even dreamed of eventual course design in places such as Dubai. Marketing experts estimated Wie's worth rocketing toward $50 million per year.

But doing those first two big deals would turn out to be a piece of cake for Berlin compared to dealing with B.J. Wie.

Michelle's father was fully invested in every single detail of his daughter's career. He had complete faith in his daughter to succeed, and he had complete faith in himself to continue his role as the leader of Wie, Inc. Because he'd laid so much groundwork with Nike and Sony, he insisted that William Morris take no cut from the two initial deals—and he got his way.

"I've been around top agents at IMG," says Gary Gilchrist, "and I would be more intimidated by B.J. Wie. He had no fear."

Most fathers of young athletes hire agents and managers in order to delegate responsibility. B.J. Wie happily delegated tasks, but he did not delegate responsibility. He was the head of the household, and his household extended to wherever his daughter went. Ross Berlin might be the newest member of Team Wie, but B.J. Wie remained team captain.

Michelle Wie appeared that week on the cover of *Fortune* magazine dressed for success in a power suit with a golf club thrown over her shoulder like a satchel. But it wasn't going to be easy being Michelle Wie. Sports contracts pay for projected future performance based on past performance. But Wie had no past performance to speak of; she was being paid for pure potential.

Her only credibility was rooted in her incredibility.

So the pressure was on to earn that money, to deliver on those high expectations. Asked by a reporter on *60 Minutes* in 2004 if she wanted to turn pro and become rich and famous, she said, "Yeah, but I think I'd like to go to high school and then go to college and be in a dorm and stuff like that. I think I just want to go through the basic steps of life, and then I think I'd be fine from then."

Everyone admires developing talent in a young person, but who admires overnight wealth in a teen? "People love you when you're not taking money," said Gilchrist. "But now the whole game has changed. Now you better back up what you say. Now she's a young girl who's got $10 million, and she's going to take a lot of pounding." There was a huge difference between an amateur who errs in the course of learning and a multimillionaire who trips up in the course of earning.

"Every time a new 'next' comes along, the sports marketing world ratchets up the hype machine," says Paul M. Swangard, of the Warsaw Sports Marketing Center. "With each new next, we're reaching an unprecedented level of anticipation and expectation thrust upon these kids. There's gotta be a point where you go off the deep end."

B.J. Wie didn't know where that point was. "I'm not a businessman," he confided to a reporter the weekend before Michelle's announcement that she was turning pro. "The only thing I've done is grade papers. I've never been in a big business negotiation before. A real estate contract is the only contract I have seen. I've been really careful there will be no mistake."

(Later he would cite that inexperience in business and financial matters as one reason he had Michelle's new riches placed in a trust fund that she couldn't touch until she was 18, and to which he and Bo had no access.)

"But you cannot be 100 percent confident," he added. "There's always potential risk."

More than he imagined.

8

Bittersweet Sixteen

Michelle Wie felt her heart thump in her chest as she stepped to the first tee in the first round of the Samsung World Championship on October 13, 2005, two days after her 16th birthday. This would be her first tee shot as a professional golfer.

She had traded her Leadbetter Academy cap for a new Nike bill. She had her name stitched into her black Sony bag. She had a full-time caddy in Greg Johnston by her side. David Leadbetter, the world's foremost golf teacher, stood close by. Greg Nared, Tiger's old friend and helper from Nike, watched her every move. So did Nike founder Phil Knight. Her new manager, Ross Berlin, was there, of course, as was a throng of reporters and photographers ready to tell her story to the world. The starter announced Wie's name and she smiled wide.

She was a pro.

Hundreds of wealthy desert denizens, Caucasian and Asian, crushed the first tee to get a glimpse of the girl's first professional swing. Some bumped into the business end of cacti; others climbed boulders to get a better view. Her first drive sailed down the fairway, and dozens of bodies bolted from around the tee, even though Wie's partner, Cristie Kerr, had yet to play her own shot. "Stand please!" became the day's anthem as the crowd ignored standard golf tournament decorum to stay as close to their new hero as possible.

The cameras followed Wie everywhere. The Golf Channel incessantly compared her to Tiger Woods. (He tied for 60th at the Greater Milwaukee Open in his pro debut in 1996.) The producers actually cut away from a still-rolling approach shot fired by another golfer to show Wie's practice swing. LPGA queen Annika Sorenstam, who owned the LPGA Tour like no other in history, shot a blistering 64, but few paid her any mind.

The cameras and her scorecard—a 2-under 70 for the day—could only suggest what Wie brought to a golf course. Her drives took off like rockets, then came to rest 20–30 yards beyond her playing partners' effort. Her irons screamed toward the pins, as if drawn by a magnetic force in each flagstick.

"What makes her different is her irons," said the AP's Doug Ferguson while walking in the media pack that followed her around the course. "It's the sound they make. A whisk. Most other shots clack. It's a bit like watching Tiger—what a sound! Forget the fashion and the age. She hits the ball differently than anyone out here."

The next day, Wie's smile was even brighter. Her limbs were loose and fluid, as if she weren't swinging at all, but merely letting her clubs blow in the breeze. She birdied the first hole with a laserlike approach shot to within 5 feet. A chip from the apron on the 3rd hole stopped within gimme length— another birdie. A pin-high approach shot on 5 yielded a third bird. As word spread, her gallery swelled.

The two-tiered green on the 7th hole, a short par 5, almost

begged to be reached in two. Wie crushed her tee shot, then pulled out a 3-wood in hopes of landing an eagle. But she blocked her shot just slightly, and her ball scooted into a lantana bush guarding the green on the right. She walked up the fairway, surveyed the situation, and quickly announced that she'd take an unplayable lie and a penalty stroke. She dropped the ball and went from going for a possible eagle to scrambling to save par. And while fans stood off to the left, elevated above the green, Wie took her stance far below the pin, able to see the flag but not the hole. She grabbed her L-wedge and hoped to stick it close.

She did. Her lob landed softly on the green and rolled directly into the hole. A huge roar went up—birdie! For a second Wie seemed as startled as everyone in the gallery by what had just happened. She just smiled and turned her hands up in a playful shrug: *Oops, I did it again!*

The next hole, a par 3, yielded another birdie. With a par on the 9th, Wie made the turn at eight strokes under for the tournament. On 11 she placed a 9-iron to within 5 feet for another birdie. Then, on the par-5 12th, she slammed a fairway wood to the green and two-putted for birdie to go 7 under for the day and 9 under for the tournament.

Wie pushed her drive on 14 to the right, and again her ball landed in a lantana bush. Wie walked quickly to the scene to find the ball nestled in the roots. Everyone in the vicinity expected her to take another unplayable. Wie stepped as close to the bush as she could and bent over at the waist so that her face hovered only inches from the shrubbery. She looked like a little girl smelling flowers, but behind the serene expression, wheels were spinning.

Time for a brief history lesson.

B.J. Wie used to keep a copy of *The Rules of Golf* beside the lounge chair in the family living room. He'd often kick up his feet after coming home from his classes at the university and flip through it. One day a few years back he found a rule that raised an eyebrow: a player is allowed free relief from any situation that threatens his or her safety. The rule book surely had something sinister in mind, like perhaps a crocodile or quicksand. But, B.J. noted, it did not define specifically what such a threatening situation might encompass, so that could be many things. . . .

Now, back to the 14th hole.

Michelle took a long look at the ball and the bush, and said something to Johnston, who called for an official. An official named Jim Haley sped over in a cart, and Wie explained her concern. Haley squatted and scanned the bush. Yes, he said, some bees were circling the flowers, but he could see no nest. He frowned. Then Wie chimed in: "I got stung by a honeybee once and my foot got all swollen."

Does a possible allergic reaction to a bee sting constitute a threat to a player's safety on the golf course? Haley evidently concluded that it did, because he ruled in favor of Michelle, who took a free drop and saved par.

Reporters promptly circled around Haley like . . . well, like bees, and came away shocked or laughing or both. They formulated their stories in their heads: *Michelle Wie knows all about the birdies and the bees.* On the next hole, B.J. listened to the chatter, smiled, and added his own play on words: "Michelle Bee! Michelle Bee!"

The minute she sat down in the media tent after her bogey-free 65, Michelle Bee was flooded with questions about the ruling on 14, so she smiled and regaled the fawning press corps with stories of her long-ago nap time run-in with a bee. Any grumbles about her exploitation of an unclear rule evaporated instantly. Wie had the reporters in stitches. She was Billy Flynn in spikes.

As the buzz continued, B.J. spoke more seriously: "Tiger once got relief from a boulder in Phoenix. Golf is funny. The rules can help you."

And sometimes they can hurt you, too.

At 9 under after two rounds, Wie was in second place, two strokes behind leader Grace Park, and so on Saturday the two teed off together.

The carefree Wie of the day before looked slightly un-nerved. The watch-this confidence she had displayed when on the tee with her driver turned into watch-out uncertainty when on the green with her putter. Her grace and ease seemed to evaporate as she lowered her lanky body over the ball.

She missed an 8-foot par putt on the third green. She walked to the ball, looked hard, and missed again. This time she stepped away, trying to calm herself. She turned her back to the ball and looked down. She deliberately went through all her pre-putt habits and missed again. She spun around as if seeking guidance, her face pale and drawn. Finally, she tapped in. She looked on the verge of panic.

As she trudged to the next tee, B.J. sidled to the cart path to wave her on. Bo, rarely vocal under any circumstance, looked toward her daughter on the next hole and shouted, "Come on, Michelle! You can do it!" Wie told Johnston she wanted to fin-ish under par for the round. She needed four birdies in the next 15 holes.

She didn't bogey another hole. She made her four birdies. And she marched off the course at minus 1 for the day. Later, she told the press, "I feel great to be in the competition. I wasn't real happy with the way I played. The third hole was pretty stupid."

A tall man with dark curly hair raised his hand. He sat in the front row of the media room, only a few feet from Wie, so she noticed him immediately. His name was Michael Bamberger, and he wrote for *Sports Illustrated.* He asked about the 7th hole, the one Wie had birdied Thursday with the perfect lob shot from beneath the elevated green. Today, she had found another bush on the same hole, and had told Park she wanted to take an unplayable lie. Park, more interested in her own shot, quickly agreed. Wie took her driver from her bag and hastily measured off two club lengths. She dropped, chipped up, two-putted for par, and moved on to the next hole.

As the gallery moved up the 8th fairway, a couple of journalists wondered aloud about the drop. It had seemed rushed. Wie hadn't requested a ruling from a tournament official this time. And most troubling, it had looked as if the ball might have been placed closer to the hole—an illegal drop.

Bamberger had waited until Wie and the gallery had moved on, then paced off the distance from the bush to the hole, and back to the site of the drop. He knew the rule book better than most because for a while it had been his job to. (Bamberger was in the process of revising his mini-classic, *The Green Road Home: A Caddie's Journal of Life on the Pro Golf Tour*, first published in 1986.) He also knew that once Wie had signed her scorecard at the end of the round, she could not add a stroke for an illegal drop. An infraction discovered after a scorecard is signed means automatic disqualification.

In the press tent, Bamberger asked about the drop. Wie explained that she had used "the triangle thing" to make sure she had dropped correctly. "I don't know," she said. "It didn't look closer." Bamberger pressed. Wie mentioned her mandate to create an "equilateral triangle"—she meant isosceles—and then laughed as she said, "I feel like I'm in geometry class!"

The room broke up—another delicious Wie moment—but Bamberger did not. He had paced one more step from the bush to the hole than from the hole to the drop. In his opinion, Wie broke the rules.

Bamberger didn't share that opinion with anybody on Saturday. He later explained that he was stuck in "reporter mode." He went back to his hotel room and the internal dialogue began. Should he alert rules officials? If they investigated and concurred with his opinion, it would mean a DQ in her first tournament as a professional. Or should he stay mum, accepting the weight of knowing he should have said something to her before she signed her scorecard and did not?

Michelle Wie slept well that night.

Michael Bamberger did not.

On Sunday, Wie sloshed through three rain delays, spending most of the day blowing birdie opportunities. She shot +2 for the day to finish at 8 under for the tournament, terrific for a rookie, especially one who had just turned 16, even if it left her in fourth place, 12 strokes behind Annika Sorenstam.

But a tournament official approached her in the scorer's tent as she was checking and signing her scorecard. He spoke to her quietly. Minutes later, Wie, Johnston, and the official took off in a cart and headed back onto the course. B.J. and Bo were walking into the media tent at that time, wet and tired. They collapsed into chairs and waited. Bo said nothing; B.J. smiled as usual and spoke of his daughter's need for more experience. Bo's extended family, in for the week from the L.A. area, huddled beneath umbrellas outside. They planned to convene at Bo's brother's house that night to celebrate, belatedly, Michelle's turning Sweet 16.

But where was Michelle?

Ross Berlin rushed in from the drizzle and leaned over to whisper in B.J.'s ear. B.J.'s face turned blank, he whispered something in Bo's ear, and they left the tent.

Reporters gathered. So did the Wie entourage out in the parking lot. What was going on? "They went to the 7th hole to look for something," said a family friend. Twenty minutes passed. Members of the press began to grouse that they had deadlines to meet and no quote from the wonder girl. LPGA officials wouldn't say a thing. Not yet.

The weather began to clear. B.J. and Bo came riding around the bend in a cart with Michelle in the back. Her shoulders sagged. Her eyes were bloodshot. She had been crying. B.J. hopped out and walked over to his extended family. He gestured and pointed in incredulity. He was upset. The looks on the Wies' faces said everything.

The rules official had told Michelle that someone—he didn't immediately say who—had questioned her drop on the 7th hole on Saturday. He asked Wie and Johnston to accompany him and a colleague to the hole. Once they got there, Michelle was asked to reenact the drop. She did so, making her best guess as to the exact spot. Johnston concurred: yes, it was there.

The rules officials paced off the distance to the hole and back. Then they used lasers to measure it. Finally, they consulted privately. Wie and Johnston, still stunned, simply waited. By then B.J. and Bo had joined the group. No one spoke.

The rules officials returned and informed Michelle of their decision: she was disqualified for having made an illegal drop and then signing an incorrect scorecard.

Michelle Wie began to cry.

B.J. raised his voice in argument, but there was no avenue for negotiation. The decision was final. Michelle, soaked from a day of rain, shivered silently in the cart, then went to the nearby house where she was staying to change into dry clothes.

Now came the first tough decision of her pro career: should she return to the media tent and face the media? B.J., Bo, Berlin, and Johnston huddled with Brian Robin, the tournament PR rep, and Paul Rovnak, the LPGA press liaison. What should she do? Berlin asked for everybody's opinion. Johnston wanted Wie to stay in the house and avoid the circus. Robin and Rovnak disagreed.

"You're dealing with a Category Two now," Robin said. "If she doesn't talk, it's a Category Five. She'll get buried." Rovnak pointed out that saying nothing gave writers a free pass to accuse Wie of cheating. "No comment" was the worst possible comment. Berlin turned to B.J., who nodded his agreement.

Fifteen minutes later, Wie entered the media tent in jeans, a white sweatshirt, and black-rimmed glasses. All week long she had looked so glamorous, so ready for prime time. Now she looked worn and beaten. Cameras snooped from every possible angle. The scene could not have diverged more from the one she had encountered back at the Kahala Mandarin, where she had announced her decision to turn pro. In Oahu, bulbs popped every time she smiled. Here they flashed the moment she looked ready to break down. She had learned the build-'em-up, tear-'em-down life of a celebrity in the span of one week.

She spoke quietly about lessons learned and putting the whole experience behind her and moving on. Next time, she vowed, she would ask for a ruling. She didn't break down. She maintained her composure. Her demeanor said, *Yes, it was disappointing, but no, it's not the end of the world.*

B.J. also kept his feelings under control. When Bamberger approached him after the press conference, Michelle's dad stuck out his hand. "Good job, Michael," he said. B.J. not only knew the rules, he also knew that in golf, spectators are encouraged to speak up when they see something untoward.

Bamberger looked down. "I don't know if it was a good job," he said.

Wie's caddy was not so forgiving. He confronted Bamberger and quietly asked why he had waited a full day to question the drop. As Bamberger muttered his side of the story, Johnston only grew more upset. Steps away, Michelle offered her explanation to a gaggle of South Korean reporters.

Then it was over. Team Wie rode away on a golf cart with Berlin and Nared hanging on to the back. They arrived late for the Sweet 16 party. They got out of the car, their bodies sagging from the ordeal and Michelle's eyes still reddened from crying. But then they entered the house, were greeted by a bunch of familiar faces, and spotted the giant cake. Michelle broke into a smile and, as if on cue, morphed back into a grinning teenager with no apparent care in the world.

B.J. and Bo, however, took the day's pains back home with them to Hawaii. They had acted with dignity, but inside they felt the sting. B.J. spun back to the series of events that had precipitated the DQ. Why had Bamberger waited so long to blow the whistle? How could he have been sure that he paced back and forth accurately?

Sports Illustrated was flooded with thousands of angry e-mails. The phones rang off the hook with complaints at the LPGA office and the USGA. Even the Royal and Ancient Golf Club issued a statement on the perceived injustice, commending Wie for her integrity and slamming Bamberger for his "mistake." SI.com hosted a Q&A with Bamberger on Thursday, which served as part apology, part rationalization. The reporter said he had attempted to do the right thing for the game and maybe even for Wie. Instead he'd made her a victim.

The week perfectly captured the Michelle Wie phenomenon. She was the biggest name in the women's game, yet she had played in just one tournament as a professional. The DQ only intensified both her fans' devotion and her skeptics' derision. Fans wanted the writer to back off. Skeptics wondered why the wonder girl was so quick to ask for an official ruling in one instance and so quick to hurry to the next shot in another.

Turning pro had changed the spotlight into a heat lamp.

Drive for Dough

The gamblers were still asleep, but the Wies were wide awake. At just before 8:00 on a brilliant October Sunday morning in Las Vegas, a black SUV pulled up to the front door of the Southern Highlands Golf Club, a few miles south of the Strip. B.J. Wie stepped out and gave a high five to Ross Berlin. Bo was with him, along with Michelle, who wore checkered pants and an orange golf sweater. It was her first public appearance since the disqualification at Samsung, but she couldn't stop smiling. She had been giddy and nervous all week in anticipation of this trip to Vegas, so much so that she couldn't concentrate on putting.

The Wies walked into the foyer and grinned at the dozen or so representatives of the media hovering on the balcony overhead. They milled about, chatting with Berlin and Greg Nared, all ready for a round. But this eighteen would differ from every one before, not just because of whom Michelle would play with, but also because her parents would stay in the clubhouse.

For the first time in Michelle's life, she would play golf without her parents watching.

A walkie-talkie blared. A palpable buzz bounced off the ornate walls. The second VIP had arrived. Michelle stood in the foyer, looking out through the open main door. B.J. stood to her left, Bo to her right. Their smiles slowly waned. Time to be serious. But Michelle couldn't. She turned to her mom, pinched her cheeks, and wiggled Bo's face side to side.

At 8:24 a.m., another SUV drew up in front and another famous golf lover climbed out. He strode through the front door, gave a big grin, and drawled, "Hullo, Mushell!" He shook B.J.'s hand and then turned to Bo, who grabbed his hand with both of hers and bowed in respect. Then he shook Michelle's hand and led her to a side room.

And there Michelle Wie spent a few minutes speaking with her playing partner for the day, former president of the United States William Jefferson Clinton.

Clinton, who was elected for his first term three weeks after Wie turned three, gave Michelle a leather-bound copy of *Golfing Memories and Methods,* by Joyce Wethered. Then he offered something else: Clinton told Wie he didn't agree with the reasons for her disqualification but admired the way she'd handled it.

Even the former leader of the Free World had a take on Michelle Wie.

The two emerged from their talk and walked upstairs. An oversized check for $500,000, made out from "Michelle Wie, Honolulu, Hawaii" to the Bush-Clinton Hurricane Relief Fund, rested against the balcony.

Clinton smiled as he told a few reporters the story of how Wie contacted him, saying he wasted no time asking for a "one-round golf lesson." Michelle then chimed in, almost whispering about how she was heartbroken to hear of the devastation in the Gulf region, and that she was "grateful to be in a position to help."

A reporter then asked, "Why is America so fascinated with Michelle?"

Clinton answered immediately: "She's a brilliant athlete, and a beautiful young woman. She's a nice person. She's a great golfer, and she puts her talents to good use, something not always done by teenagers with her gifts."

The former president paused, then went on: "Plus, pretty soon she could be winning tournaments against men."

A few more questions came, all for Clinton about his golf game, and then a final query: "Mr. President, what does Michelle represent as an Asian American?"

Clinton drew a breath, looked down, and then raised his eyes.

> She's the future of America. Hawaii is one of only two states where the majority of citizens are not of European heritage. There is no ethnic majority. That is the great gift of this country. We are held together with ideas and values. That makes it a more interesting place to be. She must be a great source of pride, pride about where we're going. Even if other nations grow to have stronger militaries and bigger economies, we still have the power of example. She represents that.

Clinton then walked to the men's locker room to put on his size 12½ Adidas golf shoes. Michelle, who looked down at the ground bashfully when Clinton spoke about her, walked downstairs to wait for him. She called a friend. "Yeah," she said into her cell, "it was pretty cool."

B.J. was much more visibly stirred. "I couldn't believe my

eyes," he said. "Michelle and the president of the United States. It is so hard to imagine. A girl from Hawaii standing with President Clinton. Incredible. We are first-generation Korean immigrants to the U.S. Just one of many. And what happened today . . ."

Clinton's golf bag, with its presidential seal, got loaded into the cart. Clinton climbed behind the wheel. Wie sat in the passenger seat and began to pepper him with questions about Hillary's potential presidential run and Chelsea's time at Stanford. The two played a full 18 under the hot desert sun, all within sight of the Strip, a beacon of everything enthralling and frightening about America's future.

The former president's score was, as always, classified as top secret.

Michelle shot 3 under.

Clinton was right: the term "Asian American" is not much older than Wie herself. When she was born in 1989, only one major newspaper—the *St. Louis Post-Dispatch*—had an Asian American as its editor. There were Asian American leaders in the United States in business, science, and academia, but few in popular culture: the media, entertainment, and politics. And Asian Americans were even rarer in sports. When ESPN compiled its list of greatest athletes of the 20th century, the number of Asian Americans who made the top one hundred was . . . zero. That's three fewer Asian Americans than horses.

Wie could change all that. "She has the opportunity to be a global citizen," said the Warsaw Sports Marketing Center's Paul Swangard. "That's where the next generation is heading already. She may be even more coveted outside our borders. There are just billions of dollars in Asia. Those markets may be ready for Michelle the way we're ready for Michelle."

But Wie had a challenge that even Michael Jordan did not face: she had to live up to a legend that had already blossomed. Almost every other athlete in the history of sports achieved dominance before he or she had influence beyond sports. Wie had influence beyond sports before she achieved. Almost every other athlete in sports history has had to live up to his or her own expectations before living up to those of the rest of the world.

Michelle Wie the golfer had to live up to Michelle Wie the icon.

Nothing better illustrates Michelle Wie's power as a marketing gold mine—and the difference between potential and performance—than her second tournament as a professional.

The Casio World Open, a regular stop on the Japan Golf Tour, always attracts a strong international field, in part because it's played in November, after the PGA Tour and European Tour seasons have wound down, and in part because of big appearance fees that lure international stars to Kochi on the island of Shikoko, two hours south of Tokyo, where the tournament has been held in recent years.

Especially eager to showcase young and fast-rising stars to represent the company's innovative side, Casio lured Tiger Woods, then just 22, to its World Open in 1998. "The company concept is creativity and making something new and good to society," tournament secretary Hiroyaki Miyazaki later explained. "It's all about trying something new, a new way of thinking."

Seven years later, for the 25th anniversary of the tournament and the 50th anniversary of the company, Casio wanted a similar draw. "We needed to get attention," Miyazaki said, "and make it really big." So Casio went after the hottest, freshest, newest, most Tiger-like attraction in golf: Michelle Wie.

Of course, when Tiger teed it up in Kochi, he had won three U.S. Junior Amateur titles, three U.S. Amateurs, and seven PGA Tour events—including his first Masters title. Michelle was still looking to add to her one trophy, from the 2003 U.S. Women's Amateur Public Links.

No one expected her to win this tournament. She was a 16-year-old girl competing against men. But that's precisely what made her appearance fee, $1.5 million, seem like a solid invest-ment to Casio. And if she made the cut? A bargain!

Casio sent a private jet to pick the Wies up. A few days be-fore leaving, B.J. had an idea for the trip. He, Bo, and Michelle went out to dinner with a family friend who spoke fluent Japanese. B.J. suggested an introduction for all the Japanese fans, to be given by Michelle, who took Japanese at school. The friend helped Michelle with the wording and the translation. And when she touched down on a November Saturday, 175 people flooded the tiny airport. They got a pleasant surprise: a greeting they understood without drawing on their second or third language. Michelle's brief speech got worldwide press.

Hundreds of camera phones clicked with Wie's every move all week. Newspapers estimated that her visit to the seaside re-sort boosted the local economy by as much as two billion yen— roughly $16 million. ("Maybe more," said Miyazaki.) The week would bring Michelle six offers of commercial deals with Asian companies, along with enough tournament invitations to Japan Tour events to fill up her entire golf calendar for a year.

She was the glittering star of the show, the number one tar-get for autograph seekers, reporters, cameras, and video crews. She could have left Kochi without swinging a club and still have qualified as the highlight of the tournament. The Casio suits got their money's worth before Wie even stuck a tee in the ground.

The old golf saw is "Drive for show, putt for dough." Well, Wie already drove for dough, plenty of it. Putting? That was another matter.

The seaside course at Kochi is long, 7,220 yards and change, and the wiry fairway grass grabs clubheads and makes shot shaping difficult. The winds off the ocean are always a big factor. But the toughest challenge for Michelle Wie came not on the tees or on the fairways, but on the greens.

Wie has always loved crushing the ball—"The best part about golf," she told Jaymes Song of the Associated Press in 2001, "is when you hit the ball long. It feels really good." But putting? Not so much. "She doesn't like to practice her putting," said Casey Nakama, her first coach. That hadn't changed much by the time she turned pro.

And it showed.

Starting on the back nine, Wie made par on each of the first six holes, hitting almost every fairway and almost every green. On the par-4 16th, Wie fired a perfect 325-yard drive and a safe iron to the short side of the green, leaving herself a tricky 25-foot uphill putt. Another par seemed likely, though, as long as she kept her first putt below the hole. If she missed long, she'd face a slippery downhill try coming back. She ran her first putt 10 feet past, missed the downhiller for par, and walked away with a three-putt bogey.

The error gnawed at Wie. Her eyes narrowed and her jaw set. She folded her arms. This was, almost invariably, how Wie appeared when bothered. She blocked her drive on 17 to the right, then dropped her head like a child sent to her room. And on 18, she smashed her drive on a 530-foot par 5 (which plays more like 600 yards with its uphill slope) to the middle of the fairway, hit a long iron all the way to the apron, and then chipped to within 8 feet. Three fine shots, but then she missed her makeable birdie putt and had to settle for a par.

By now, one thing was abundantly clear: no matter the length of the course, this 16-year-old girl would have no trouble driving with the men.

But another thing became equally clear: for now, at least, Michelle Wie would have trouble scoring with them because of her putting.

In tournaments on the Japan Tour, it's customary for players to take a 30-minute break at the turn. They repair to the clubhouse, grab a bite, and rest before going back out to finish their round. Wie, still fuming over her lone bogey, didn't relish the respite. She sat in the players' lounge and silently stewed.

The second half of her round soon added to her frustration. She yanked her tee shot on the 2nd hole, a par 3, and left herself a 60-foot chip. Then, as if she had been doing it for 40 years instead of 10, she lifted a soft chip over a swale and rolled it to within 3 feet. Leadbetter was beside himself: "No LPGA player can hit a shot like that!"

Wie missed the easy par putt.

On the next hole, a variation on the same tune: gorgeous drive, slightly errant approach, good chip, missed putt—another bogey. On the 4th hole (her 13th of the day) she stared for what seemed like minutes at a straight 6-foot putt that by then must have looked more like 6 miles. Finally, she stepped up and dropped the putt, her head dropping in relief.

An odd sight: a 16-year-old girl, playing against adult men, depending on her long game to shore up her short game. On the 7th, she covered 620 yards in three sizzling shots, and then—perhaps invigorated by what she'd just done—made the birdie putt. She finished her first round at 73, 1 over par.

"If I make a couple more putts," she said in the press room afterward, "I'm all set."

Japan didn't care about Wie's putting problems. More than 4,000 fans showed up to line the fairways, and few expected more than a glimpse at one of the world's most perfect swings. "She's wonderful," raved Japanese pro Taichi Teshima, who was in her group. "A couple of bad chips, a couple of bad putts, but her shots are almost the same length as ours. I think she'd make a card here, easy." A Japanese reporter named Yoshi Akiyama put it in plainer terms: "This is our one chance to see her. And she is beautiful. Look at all the men here."

Michelle Wie was everything the Japanese loved about golf and everything Japanese men loved about women: feminine yet powerful, fragile yet intimidating. By the late 1990s women's golf in Japan had surpassed the men's game in appeal. A short, compact dynamo named Ai Miyazato was almost as common a sight on billboards and subway posters as any baseball player.

"The larger-than-life is much bigger here," said Dean Harvey, a Nike rep based in Japan. "With heroes, it's respect and awe. The challenge is trying to keep her special."

Back in the States, another Michelle Wie believer watched the first round of the Casio with the same interest but a lot more concern.

Tony Kewalramani was a California-based putting coach who had worked with Wie briefly back in 2002, when Michelle was 12 and practicing for her first Kraft Nabisco Championship. He remembers seeing the Wies pull up in their rented minivan. He saw Bo get out of the car and thought: *She's tall.*

Then he saw B.J. get out of the car and thought: *He's really tall.* Finally, he saw two long legs unfold and hit the pavement, and Michelle climbed out. The putting coach thought: *Wow!*

But could she putt? Kewalramani took Wie out to the practice green. Michelle demonstrated an easy, fluid motion. No locked joints, no hunched back, no death grip on the putter. And, as the putting coach soon found out, she was as aggressive on the greens as she was on the tee box.

To see how Michelle reacted to pressure and payoff, Kewalramani dropped a ball 30 feet from the hole and announced that this putt would be worth $20—not a bad incentive for a 12-year-old. Michelle eyed the line, stepped up, and snaked it in. She giggled.

The coach smiled. Then he announced: double or nothing. Michelle's eyes widened. This time, Kewalramani dropped a ball 40 feet away, with a vicious left-to-right break in between the girl and the prize. Michelle lined it up, eyed it, and guided the putter head through the ball. The putt started left and slowly moved right . . . right . . . right . . . and *clunk.*

This time Michelle laughed out loud. B.J. beamed. And Tony Kewalramani got goose bumps.

By the end of that first day, Kewalramani looked straight into B.J.'s eyes and echoed to the word the conclusion Gary Gilchrist had previously come to: "If she doesn't win a major by sixteen, I will be shocked."

Kewalramani took a coaching job at UCLA, so the teacher-student relationship ended, but he remained a devoted Wie-watcher. In 2005, he tuned in to the Samsung tournament and marveled once again at how his former student handled so much attention and still blistered drives so far past all the competition. But when she got to the greens, Kewalramani noticed that Michelle Wie didn't putt the way she had years before.

She was stiff. She froze over the ball. She was mechanical

rather than fluid. To Kewalramani, she looked completely uncomfortable.

Trouble on day 2 at the Casio began early. Wie's tee shot on the second hole drifted slightly to the right, and a mediocre approach left her 70 feet away from the hole on a humpbacked green reminiscent of an 18th hole on a miniature golf course. Three putts. Bogey.

Next hole: another huge green, another so-so approach, 40 feet away. Wie jabbed at the ball on her first putt, with no follow-through at all. Three putts. Bogey.

That set the pattern for the day. Long drives that found the fairway. Iron shots that never veered into traps or water or even deep rough. Approaches that ranged from adequate to good. But with the putter in her hands . . . well, on the greens in the second round of the 2005 Casio World Golf Open, Michelle Wie putted like a blindfolded dart thrower trying to hit the bull's-eye.

Wie's stare would have melted steel as she walked off the 9th for her "rest break" with three bogeys on her scorecard, all the result of inept putting. Word from the clubhouse drifted to her gallery: the cut would likely be +3. Wie stood at +2. That was the good news. The bad news was that the greens were hardening and quickening.

Even so, Wie looked confident when she teed off on 10. A birdie brought out a relieved smile. A run of pars left her looking positively ebullient as she walked off the 16th green. Two more pars and she would make the cut—and history.

Seventeen was a disaster. Decent drive, but her approach scooted through the green into gnarly rough. On her chip, the grass grabbed her L-wedge and the ball limped only halfway to the hole. Visibly upset—a punch with a long iron would have been a smarter play—she crouched and eyed the 20 feet remaining for an eternity. Finally, she stood up and walked to the ball. She stood over it, looked at the hole, looked down at her ball, readied, and . . . a cell phone rang.

Wie stepped away, exasperated. Fans stared daggers at the perp. Wie returned to her ball, stroked it, and watched it slide past. Bogey. She walked to the par-5 18th at 3 over for the tournament, right on the cut line.

There she encountered a traffic jam. The group ahead hadn't even teed off yet. Finally, after stewing in her thoughts for 20 minutes, she made her only bad drive of the day. Not just bad. Terrible. She blocked it far right, and her ball came to rest half buried behind a tree, leaving her no option but to punch out sideways into the fairway, which left her 140 yards to the green. Her third shot came up short of the green. She needed to get up and down to save par and make the cut. Her chip, like all her other chips in the last two days, was only decent, leaving her what she read as an 8-foot right-to-left putt. No gimme, but makeable.

She stepped up to her ball, took a deep breath, and stroked the ball exactly at the spot she'd picked. The ball rolled exactly on the line she'd selected and then, at the last second, veered right and slid past the hole.

Misread.

Bogey.

Michelle Wie stared at her ball in shock and covered her mouth with her hand. She couldn't believe what she'd just seen.

She slid down in her chair in the media tent and turned her toes inward like a child awaiting a visit to the principal's office. She tried to make herself small, not easy if you're 6'1". Her voice wavered, but only slightly, as she began answering questions.

"Things just didn't work out today. . . ."

"The six bogeys were pretty stupid. . . ."

"The last two holes . . . shouldn't have happened."

She admitted to being "a little bit nervous," which in Wie-speak meant a lot nervous. Then she added wistfully, "I don't know if it proves anything that I almost made the cut."

Michelle Wie came to the Casio World Golf Open, her second outing as a professional, with high expectations. In her eyes, she had come up short. Never mind that those expectations were crazy high, way beyond reasonable. She had come up short, period.

Worse still, and it wouldn't be confirmed until down the road, she had a putting problem that wouldn't go away.

Despite the immediate disappointment, Ross Berlin flew directly from Japan to Korea and had no trouble locking in another tournament appearance against men in Seoul set for the following May. He also negotiated sponsorship deals, one with a pharmaceutical company and another with a noodle maker. Turned out that nobody in Asia cared much whether Michelle Wie made bogey or par on the last hole of the Casio World Open.

Back home, though, Wie entered a new phase of scrutiny. Now she would be judged on her performance as a golfer, not her promise as a prodigy. Standards were shifting. The perfect swing, however beautiful, and the distance from the tee, however remarkable, weren't enough anymore. Her next tournament was the Sony Open in January, where she had rocked the world the in year 2004.

Time to make good on all the hype.

Time to make a cut.

10

Gentlemen Only ...

Michelle Wie spent the 2005 Christmas holidays working on her putting, which needed it, but she devoted at least as many hours to the one part of her game that didn't appear to have a single flaw: her swing.

For all her fame as a teenage boomer off the tee, B.J. Wie knew his daughter didn't have quite the distance to compete on the PGA Tour. Two days before she turned pro, he told a reporter, "She wants to boost her distance by 10 percent over the next three years. Right now her average carry distance is 260. To compete on the PGA Tour, she has to go at least 285. At least."

The extra 10 percent, B.J. figured, would come from two sources. The first was a famous name in the golf world: teacher to the stars David Leadbetter. The second was an unknown (at least in golf circles), Canadian kinesiologist Paul Gagné.

* * * * *

David Leadbetter is so admired worldwide by golfers that he can't appear on any course without having to sign at least a half dozen autographs. His wide-brimmed hat is as iconic in the golf world as Greg Norman's shark logo. Born in England, he played without success on the European and South African tours in the early 1970s before moving on to teaching. Over a decade his thoughts and observations coalesced into a holistic theory on golf's greatest and most elusive mystery: the perfect golf swing.

"David Lead" started the David Leadbetter Golf Academy in 1983; there are now 30 branches in 13 nations. Among his students over the last 25 years: Nick Faldo, Greg Norman, Nick Price, Seve Ballesteros, Curtis Strange, and Ernie Els. His seven tutorial books have sold more than two million copies.

Leadbetter is also the inventor of a swing aid called the Swing Setter. His Web site promises that the device is "the closest thing to a lesson with David." (And it can be yours for only $99.99, plus tax and shipping.) Here's a partial description:

> Develops your Grip, Swing Plane, Release and Tempo—the four keys to a great golf swing. A perfect training tool for golfers of every level who want to improve but either don't have the time or are simply practicing the wrong things. Using the Swing Setter as little as six minutes, twice a week will give you the understanding and feel for a great golf swing. You'll gain power, accuracy and above all else, consistency. Use it at home, in the office or on the practice range—you'll be completely amazed. It's simple, fun, addicting . . . and it works!

Maybe it does, maybe it doesn't, but Leadbetter introduced the Swing Setter to Wie at around the same time he took it to the marketplace. Was he trying to improve on perfection? Not exactly. At the time, Wie had a relatively shallow swing plane, so she came down to the ball more like a 747 landing than like a hammer dropping. Her follow-through was so long and easy, and it looked so beautiful, and the results were usually so good, that the top PGA and LPGA pros who got to know her a little bit told her never to mess with it.

But Wie practiced with the Swing Setter, and listened to its inventor, and slowly but surely her backswing arc got a bit steeper and her follow-through got a little tighter. Presto—perfection got a little more perfect.

On the range, Wie began checking her driver practice swings halfway up, looking back to eye her alignment, and then continuing to the apex of the backswing. That was to make sure the arms were finished and the upper body could take over. The act looked mechanical—the exact opposite of the fluid Big Wiesy swing—but that was on purpose. The idea was to make the swing more powerful and compact and repeatable. Under pressure situations on the course, Wie's looseness could backfire: her clubface could come to impact open or closed, and all that power would only push or pull her drives astray.

Leadbetter hoped to keep the power, strengthen it, and make it more consistent. To do so, he was breaking an almost automatic whole into practiced parts. Some observers thought Leadbetter was trying to fix something that wasn't broken.

A short but powerful man with a background in hockey and weightlifting, Paul Gagné believes fervently in the interrelationship of balance, mind, and strength. He fit well as a mentor for Wie, as she had a rare sense of balance, amazing flexibility, and an acute physical awareness. A French Canadian, Gagné had worked mostly with hockey players before meeting her, and he observed that the best in that sport showed the same mind-body coordination Wie had.

But there was a big difference.

"So many players are dumb as a hockey stick," Gagné said after he started working with Michelle. "With her, it's the opposite. She learns in 15 minutes what most people wouldn't be able to learn in a week. She's also very disciplined. And her nervous system is very good."

Wie has very powerful legs, so she didn't need much help there. Gagné wanted to strengthen her core and her upper body to help Leadbetter's efforts to make Wie's swing more compact and powerful. It worked: Wie gained a club in her iron play within two months of starting with Gagné in May 2004.

There were just two risks.

The first was bulk. Wie was so flexible that her follow-through carried her shoulders almost to the point where her toes faced in one direction and her neck faced the opposite. Her height, combined with her turn, gave her a stunning double whammy that no other female player had. Adding muscle could potentially decrease that turn.

The second was strain. Wie had long arms, enormous hands, and strong hips and legs. All that torque put enormous stress on her wrists, which had to flex and release over and over again. Added strength and added practice always involved the risk of injury. And Wie had first hurt her left wrist even before she met Gagné in 2004, when she struck a rock on a downswing.

"Michelle had problems with her left wrist for the last three years," Gagné said in 2007. "She never had the strength in her wrists compared to her body. As soon as we tried to get her wrists strong, she had inflammation. She creates so much leverage and so much speed. So we got her back strong, her abdominals, everything, no problem. Now her only problem was her wrists."

Leadbetter's Swing Setter device made her swing even more "handsy," which in turn put more pressure on her wrists. A close friend of the Wie family advised B.J. to drop the swing aid, but Michelle, ever the perfectionist, ever the worker bee, used the swing aid so much that she started swinging it more than real clubs.

Gagné flew out to Honolulu in December 2005 to work with Michelle. He put her through so many upper-body exercises that she couldn't lift her arms to massage shampoo through her hair. Somehow she would have to strike a balance between strength and strain, between work and overwork.

Ira Helfer loves hot dogs. He loved them when he was a kid growing up in Chicago. He kept on loving them after he ended a successful career in the international housewares business and bought a retirement home along the first fairway of the Waialae Country Club in 1981.

A former winner of the Sony Pro-Am, he's something of a local legend, but not for his good golf game. He's famous for the franks he grills and serves to friends who drop by his back-yard next to the 10th tee during the Sony Open. That's because over the years he's made enough "friends" to start his own Face-book: fans attracted by the smoky aroma, journalists always on the lookout for a free meal, caddies, and, in the last few years, players looking for a quick protein boost. (Fred Funk and Mark O'Meara are regulars.) During the 2006 Sony Open, Helfer served up more than 1,200 free hot dogs.

But one person wouldn't have been able to get an Ira Helfer hot dog at any price: Michelle Wie. "She can't get one here," Helfer said. "I only give 'em to people I like."

Helfer doesn't believe women have any place on the PGA Tour. He didn't like it when Annika Sorenstam played the Colonial in 2003, and he didn't like Michelle Wie playing the Sony. Nothing personal. He just believes women should play against women, and men should play against men.

"That's the normal way of doing things," he said before the 2006 event got under way. "She's a 16-year-old girl phenom who hasn't won anything. Soon enough, she's going to be a 19-year-old nothing who still hasn't won anything. She'll have a big collection of chandelier earrings."

So at the 2006 Sony, Helfer hung out in his backyard during tournament week, grilled dogs, and watched the participants putt out on the 9th hole, but he turned away when Wie came up the fairway. "I don't watch her," he said. "I don't like her. She doesn't belong there. So I don't look."

Ira Helfer wasn't alone.

A teenage girl who has not won a professional tournament should not be playing against professional men.

That was the underlying feeling among card-carrying members of the PGA Tour, though most wouldn't say so for the record. More likely they would smile when asked if they thought she should be allowed to play, let out a sigh, then dodge the direct question with something like "She brings people out to the tournaments" or "She builds atmosphere."

"Some people are too scared to say anything," said Australian John Senden, who would go on later to win the 2006 John Deere Classic, where Wie missed the cut. "A lot of guys worry about her beating them. Maybe it's an embarrassment thing."

Pros were amused by the Wie novelty in 2004, but two years later many vented (off the record) that Wie insulted them by thinking she could beat them regularly without first beating the best women in the world. They bristled that the top PGA Tour golfers, like Tiger Woods and Vijay Singh, would never have to deal with the media circus of two rounds with Wie, because she was always paired with players from the bottom of the money list. These were the guys who desperately needed to make cuts and leave with a paycheck as they struggled to keep their Tour cards. They had to handle the distraction and the pressure of playing against a teenage girl, and they didn't like it one bit. Also, every sponsor's exemption that Michelle Wie got meant one less available to young male pros aching for a chance to prove themselves.

"In the locker room," said one such player, anonymously, "a lot of guys will tell you they want her to shoot 100 and never come back."

Some Tour members even went on the record.

CHRIS DiMARCO (*three PGA Tour wins though 2008; turned pro in 1990*): "She's a tremendous talent. Phenomenal. I can't believe she's even thinking about doing this. But I'd like to see her beat the best girls her age, and win on the LPGA Tour."

RYAN PALMER (*two PGA Tour wins; turned pro in 2000*): "My whole goal is to win a golf tournament. I want to win, not just make a cut. She's good, no doubt about that. Definitely mature. But she doesn't have the pressure some of us do."

DAN CHOPRA (*two PGA Tour wins; turned pro in 1992*): "If I was as good as her, I'd try to be the greatest women's golfer who ever lived. She has the opportunity to do that. And she's squandering it by wasting her time out here. It's a shame she's wasting an opportunity to become the greatest ever. She wasn't even one of the top 10 amateurs of all time. People play for records. Records make you go down in history. People remember Bobby Jones for that—for the records."

K.J. CHOI (*seven PGA Tour wins; turned pro in 1994*): "She has a great game, and a great swing, but she needs more experience. She should go to Q-school."

FRED FUNK (*eight PGA Tour victories; turned pro in 1981*): "Nobody belongs who doesn't qualify. You go to Q-School or earn enough to get a card. Does she belong? Absolutely not. My advice is to be the best woman out there. If you are, then come out here. She is a great role model, a great marketing tool, but she hasn't earned her way."

TAG RIDINGS (*no PGA Tour wins; turned pro in 1997*): "She has tons of potential, and I hope to see her do well. My advice? Make some putts, baby."

Just two years earlier, the likes of Ernie Els, Tom Lehman, and Paul Azinger had raved about Wie, praising her swing, her potential, and her likely impact on golf. But in only 24 months, the Wie glow had faded. The 2006 Sony Open was only the fourth PGA Tour event Wie had played in, yet many people had grown weary of her story, maybe because they'd expected her to make the cut sooner.

Perhaps this was a by-product of Wie's continued excellence on the women's tour—by the end of 2005, she had four top-10 finishes in LPGA majors. Perhaps it was a consequence of chauvinism finally breaking through. Perhaps it was both. Whatever the mix, Wie playing against the guys wasn't so adorable anymore.

Michelle also had to balance real life and golf life. She had a driving test—cars, not golf—scheduled for the following Tuesday after the Sony, and she had a school test and a paper to deal with. She was on another mini-diet, hoping to keep her New Year's resolutions to "cut down on sugar" and be "not as lazy." Meanwhile, she was playing 9 holes at Waialae three times a week and 18 holes twice on the weekends.

Asked about being a pro and still a high school student, Wie said, "A part of me wants to play every week. Another part wants to be normal. That's a part of my life I don't think I could live without."

Wie seemed to be feeling more pressure the fourth time around at the Sony. Her Pro-Am round went poorly. Wie seemed agitated throughout and said little to her corporate playing partners. Her group's score was the worst on Wednesday's board.

Her Thursday group looked like the story of golf's past, present, and future. Wie was matched with Chris Couch, a dip-chewing, paunchy 32-year-old ball crusher in shades who was trying to hang on to his Tour card, and Camilo Villegas, a 24-year-old rising star from Colombia who would end up on *People* magazine's "Most Beautiful People" list for the year. (He would go on to log two wins in 2008, one of them the TOUR Championship, to make good on his early celebrity.) On the first hole, the 10th, Wie split the fairway while both Couch and Villegas mishit their drives. A man's scream—"You go, girl!"—reverberated through the gallery.

Wie made par on 10 and again on 11. Then came 12 and a scene eerily familiar to Wie's struggles with her putter in Japan.

She made a perfect drive on the par-4, 446-yard hole, watching it come to rest 300 yards away. Her approach, into a right-to-left breeze, found the back fringe. She walked to the green, which backed up against a wall and a local street. Across the road, two shirtless fans stood on a lava rock wall to get a look. Wie punched her 25-foot putt to within 3 feet and an apparent third par. But she pulled the putt left.

After the bogey, Wie yanked her next drive into the left rough. She hurried to the ball, took out a wood, put it back, took it out again, and then proceeded to hook the ball into deeper rough. Her approach landed short of the green, and she misread her putt for bogey. Suddenly Wie was 3 over and staring at a lost weekend only an hour into her first round.

Then, after squeaking out a par on 14, she pushed her approach shot into a bunker on 15. Wie flew the green from there, let out a big sigh, then stared blankly out at the horizon after holing out for another double bogey. She was +5 after six holes. Another double, three more bogeys, and a birdie—*yes!*—later, she finished the round at +9.

One reason for the catastrophe is that she stopped listening to her caddy. Wie had come to believe that she should ignore middle-aged men on the course, in the media, and even Ira Helfer behind the fence by the 10th fairway. But she was also not listening to the middle-aged man she employed to help her win. Johnston had worked the LPGA circuit longer than Wie had been alive, helping Juli Inkster to one of the most successful careers in women's golf history. Inkster had won 30 LPGA tournaments and 7 majors, with Johnston reading her putts during the most productive 16 seasons of her 21 years on the LPGA Tour. But Team Wie decided early in the season that Johnston would not assist Michelle in reading greens. Instead, she would consult only the thick notebook B.J. filled with notes and sketches and arrows.

"We decided Michelle cannot depend on her caddy. She has to learn from her mistakes," B.J. told the press later in the season. "We're not going to have the caddy help her read greens. She will never become a great player if she doesn't learn from her mistakes."

The 9 over on Thursday at the Sony was the worst round of her first professional season. Standing just off the final green, Leadbetter said, "Best-laid plans sometimes go awry. She's a pro now, here under a microscope. Should she play, shouldn't she play? It'll make her tougher. If this was the LPGA Tour, 5 over would be leading."

AP writer Doug Ferguson asked Wie after the round, "What did you learn today?"

"I haven't really digested it yet," she said. "Things didn't go the way I wanted them to. I can't believe I'm doing this bad."

She looked like she was about to cry.

Her putting hadn't improved since Japan. She still couldn't read greens, even on her own home course. And now her confidence was shaken. "You kinda start doubting yourself," she said. "You think it's going to break one way, then it breaks another way."

A rookie playing different greens on different tours on different continents in different months might be expected to struggle with putting. Greens on PGA Tour courses get cut differently than LPGA Tour greens, so that only added to the confusion. Wie had plenty of good reasons to explain her performance. But every mistake at a PGA Tour event became another reason for critics to insist she should be staying on the women's circuit.

Friday was another day.

Michelle made five bogeys, mostly a result of poor putting, but she also made seven birdies in a roller-coaster 2-under round that thrilled just about everyone on the property except Ira Helfer. Sure, she missed the cut by four strokes, but . . . was she getting closer?

"She was just awesome," said Villegas, who'd noticed Wie's anxiety the day before and tried to reassure her after the round. "She inspired me. She *will* make a cut in a men's event. It must be so hard to be in her shoes."

"Everybody has to be patient," B.J. said on Friday after his daughter's wild, gutsy round. "I'm confident. I know it will come."

But would it come fast enough?

Could Michelle Wie ever live up to the multimillion-dollar bets her sponsors had placed on her?

And, more important, would she ever live up to her own great expectations for herself?

11

Five Points

The Wies had visitors in February. Steve Kroft and a crew from *60 Minutes* came to Hawaii for a follow-up on the story he'd done on Wie in 2004. Kroft wanted to sit down and interview Michelle in much the same way he had two years before. The subject and the questions were basically the same, but this story would be quite different.

The first show had aired on April 11, 2004, immediately after CBS's final-round coverage of the Masters. That was no coincidence. Kroft asked Wie, then fairly new as a celebrity, to describe her "ultimate goal." Wie said she wanted to play in the Masters. She said that "it'd be pretty neat walking down the Masters fairways." Then Kroft asked if Wie would like to win the Masters. "Yeah, I'd love to," she said. "But I think the green jacket's a little bit out of fashion."

Kroft had asked if Wie wanted to "push the envelope." Wie replied that she didn't know what that meant. Kroft explained, and then Wie said: "I like challenges. . . . I always have to be the first to do everything."

Michelle had called herself "freakishly tall" and said she didn't want to grow any more. She said playing women's tournaments over and over again might make her "bored with golf." She said growing up with her dad taught her that "men's egos can be easily brought down." And she said she wanted to go through high school and college before turning pro.

Wie had come off as fresh and candid. Already some said the 14-year-old was merely her parents' puppet, but her honesty—even about her parents' shortcomings—showed otherwise. Wie could sound bratty, but her giggle seemed too innocent to condemn. To many inside and outside of the game who saw golf as too old, too male, and too staid, this young girl looked like she could shake things up a bit.

The second *60 Minutes* segment aired April 9, 2006, almost exactly two years later. This time, her parents and three William Morris representatives watched her on a monitor in the next room. Michelle looked more reserved, even careful. She didn't laugh as easily, didn't volunteer nearly as many opinions, didn't joke as much.

Kroft asked about her new management group, and Wie said, "It feels nice to have, you know, people that you can trust around you." Kroft asked if Wie could "feel" the fame she had achieved. Her answer to Kroft was a simple no. Kroft responded in surprise: "No?" Wie replied, "Not really. I don't know."

Wie loosened up some during the next segment, when she called her housework skills "pathetic" and said marrying at 16 "might be illegal." But overall, viewers learned less about the 16-year-old Michelle Wie on *60 Minutes* than they had about the 14-year-old edition two years before.

• • • • •

Remaining aloof and apart had served Michelle well for most of her brief time in the spotlight. She rarely responded directly to criticism, implied or otherwise. But this attitude was perplexing to many, who felt she rationalized everything. Others saw her as above-it-all, self-enabling, or simply uninterested in outside opinion.

"Michelle is a phenomenal talent," LPGA Hall of Famer Beth Daniel, now an analyst for the Golf Channel, told a reporter for the *Asbury Park Press* in New Jersey. "But there are players out there that are also phenomenal talents, who don't get the press that she gets because with her it's always been about the media and making decisions that kind of spotlight her in the media."

Wie did little to defuse such feelings, saying publicly only that she idolized Tiger Woods and not Annika Sorenstam. B.J. had also said that Michelle wanted to master the LPGA by age 20. Wie was always excited to play LPGA events, but because she tuned out all the criticism, she never nipped the suspicion that she looked down on (or beyond) the women's tour.

The LPGA, meanwhile, embraced Wie when convenient and shooed her away when expedient. When commissioner Carolyn Bivens asked players to sign pin flags to thank Rolex for its support as a sponsor, she included a flag for Wie to sign, even though Michelle wasn't a member and was sponsored by Rolex's rival.

In February 2006, when the first-ever Rolex World Rankings came out, Wie grabbed all the headlines for being ranked third despite the fact that she had made a grand total of zero dollars on the LPGA Tour the previous year. Wie was only a fraction of a point behind 2005 Louise Suggs Rolex Rookie of the Year Paula Creamer, who'd made 24 out of 25 cuts the previous season, won twice, ranked third overall in scoring average, and earned more than $1.5 million. (Asked about all the Wie hype, Creamer shrugged and said, "I'm used to it.")

The rules declared that "players who have not yet been included in the Rolex Rankings may be included after having played in eight eligible events over a 52-week period." That minimum strangely coincided with the number of LPGA Tour events Wie, as a nonmember who depended on sponsors' exemptions, was allowed to enter each year. Chris Higgs, technical director of the Rolex Rankings, insisted that the suggestion that the divisor was originally placed at 15 and then lowered to make room for Wie was "simply not true."

Wie was "flabbergasted" by the rankings—and obviously sensitive to the suggestion that the rules had been rigged in her behalf. "It's not like I invented them," she told reporters. "It's not like I put myself in number three. It's not like I woke up one day and said, 'Okay, why don't I be number three in the world?' All I did was play golf."

"Michelle's a great girl," Cristie Kerr told *USA Today*. (Kerr had six LPGA Tour wins in 2005 and finished two notches below Wie in the Rolex Rankings.) "She's had great success, but she hasn't made a dollar on our tour. It seems odd how they came up with this."

The Kraft Nabisco Championship, formerly the Colgate Dinah Shore, is the first major of the LPGA season, and it always caps off its week with a wall-shaking party. After the champion does her traditional dive into the lake surrounding the 18th island green, the main clubhouse fills up with hundreds of women. A DJ starts pumping music, and the women—many in their thirties and forties, white and with short hair—crowd onto a makeshift dance floor and rock the room for hours. The gathering gets so large that partygoers routinely use the men's bathroom.

Rightly or wrongly, women's sports are often viewed by male sports fans as a haven for lesbians. Golf is no different, as the LPGA has rarely been seen as "feminine," flashy, or sexy. (One nickname: the "Lesbians Playing Golf Association.") And since men dominate sports viewership, ratings and purses lag well behind PGA numbers. Tiger Woods' arrival on the scene in the late 1990s only widened the gap. The LPGA had no must-see players back then who could appeal to young women or 18-to-35-year-old men.

Other sports had attractive yet powerful American female icons, such as Mia Hamm, Marion Jones, Cynthia Cooper, Danica Patrick, and Laila Ali. The LPGA star of similar stature was Annika Sorenstam. And so women's sports headlines went to the Women's World Cup team, the Olympic softball team, the college basketball darlings at Connecticut and Tennessee, and the WNBA.

Ty Votaw arrived as LPGA commissioner in 1999, and his first big job was to preside over the LPGA's 50th anniversary in 2000. As he was doing so, he quietly worried about the LPGA's fixation with tradition. Six months into 2000, he thought, *This is all about the past.*

But almost overnight, that changed. And it changed for reasons that Votaw himself didn't immediately embrace.

Early in 2003, Votaw got a call from Mark Steinberg, the player representative from IMG. Steinberg represented Sorenstam, who in 2001 became only the second non-American to win at Kraft since the championship became a major in 1983. (Helen Alfredsson of Sweden won in 1993.) Steinberg told Votaw that Sorenstam had an idea: she wanted to play in a PGA Tour tournament. Would the commissioner mind?

Votaw blanched. First and foremost, Sorenstam's effort

would certainly direct attention away from that week's LPGA Tour event. How would sponsors feel about that? Second, what if she played poorly? What would that say about the quality of play on his tour?

Michelle Wie had declared her intention to play in men's events years before, but she'd been a kid, and years away from playing full-time in the LPGA. Sorenstam was the best female player in the world. Votaw wondered: how could this possibly be good for the Tour? And it didn't help that respected players, whom Votaw will not name, asked him how he could dare allow Sorenstam to skip out of a tour stop to play against men.

But Sorenstam soothed Votaw's nerves by promising him that she was only doing this to improve herself. As Votaw himself said, "Who can argue with that?"

Sorenstam's first round at the 2003 Colonial in Fort Worth was, quite simply, one of the most memorable moments in women's sports history. The press coverage was intense, as was the reaction of the PGA Tour, including naysayers such as Vijay Singh, who said Sorenstam should not be out with the men for so much as a single round.

Pinnacle Sports, an online betting service, placed odds on Sorenstam making the cut and saw as much action as on a typical NFL Sunday game. Mobs flooded the venerable Fort Worth course, carrying GO ANNIKA! signs and creating the types of galleries normally reserved for Tiger Woods. After ramping up her driving distance in the months prior with an intense workout regimen, Sorenstam hit a perfect tee shot off the 10th tee on a Thursday, watched it sail straight ahead and land in the fairway, and half collapsed in mock relief as she walked off the tee box. That not only endeared her to golf fans, it also changed her public identity from "Sorenstam" to "Annika." In a sport known for players Jack, Tom, Arnie, and Tiger, the women finally had a one-word name of their own.

Annika missed the cut by four strokes with a two-day total of 145 (5 over), but she had made a statement for herself and for women athletes. She wanted to play against the men for the same reason Wie did—to play against the best in her sport and learn. Yet by 2006, when Michelle Wie missed her third Sony Open cut, she was being widely criticized for, in effect, not knowing "her place." Votaw pointed out the difference, saying, "Annika did it once."

Did Annika hurt the LPGA Tour by playing Colonial?

Or was the occasional effort by one of their stars to beat the men just what the women's game needed to boost its Q rating?

No one could possibly argue that Michelle Wie didn't bring exposure to the women's game. How many other female golfers had been on David Letterman's show before the age of 15? No one could argue her ability to perform; she had finished near the top of the leaderboard in all four majors at the age of 16. No one could argue that she didn't draw fans, media attention, and sponsor attention and sponsors like no one else in the history of women's golf.

Exposure? She was only one of the most photographed athletes in the world.

Wie fit perfectly into Commissioner Votaw's "Five Points of Celebrity" program—Performance, Approachability, Passion, Appearance, Relevance—that he formulated in 2002 to guide the LPGA. He carefully did not insist that a golfer belong to the LPGA; he used the term "professional/member." His "brand promise" was to "showcase the best in women's professional golf." And he had a strong and decidedly modern view on the direction women's professional golf had to take: "The LPGA is competing not just in the golf industry but also in the sports entertainment industry. Our success and our members' success will be determined by how well the LPGA meets consumers' entertainment interests."

Michelle Wie was the Five Points of Celebrity come to life.

Critics within the LPGA said that she siphoned off fans when she went off-circuit, but Wie supporters countered that her forays onto the men's tours, here and abroad, garnered attention and recruited new fans. For instance, an opening montage of a major Korean television network's coverage of an LPGA Tour event featured highlights of Michelle Wie, who was—is—immensely popular in Korea. So what if she wasn't a member of the LPGA?

"What I couldn't understand," says Gary Gilchrist, "is here's someone who's coming along that's bringing attention, and you tell them to stay in Hawaii. I thought it was sad. This is so good for your sport. You should learn from the Tiger example."

Carolyn Bivens took over as LPGA commissioner—the first female in the organization's history—in July 2005 when Votaw stepped down. (In 2006 he was named executive VP for international affairs of the PGA Tour.) She said that Wie was popular "for exactly the same reason Procter & Gamble and Johnson & Johnson put out new products: we want something new. We're always interested in what's next."

The first round of the 2006 Kraft Nabisco saw a pairing that must have made the author of the Five Points of Celebrity stand up and cheer: Michelle Wie, 16, playing in her first major since turning pro, and Ai Miyazato, 20, an LPGA rookie who had won 15 times on Japan's LPGA Tour.

The younger golfer had been around for a while. The older was the new kid on the block.

The younger possessed a swing of classic beauty. The older displayed one that was unorthodox but visually arresting: a backswing that eked upward slowly, as if she were a Hollywood ax murderer ready to kill, her downswing a torrent.

The younger had not even sought to get her Tour card after turning pro. The older had made her bones on the LPGA of Japan Tour, then dominated the Q-School this side of the Pacific to earn her LPGA Tour card.

Miyazato came to America after winning the hearts of millions of golf-crazy Japanese men and women. Her popularity in Japan was akin to that of baseball stars Ichiro Suzuki and Hideki Matsui. Women's golf in Japan had surpassed men's golf in popularity mainly because of Ai, who had dozens of reporters following her even as she played half a world away from home in the United States. Half of the crowd in LPGA media tents were American journalists there to cover an event, and the other half were Japanese journalists there to cover Miyazato.

And Miyazato, like Wie, took a turn against men. Only weeks after Wie missed the cut in Kochi in November 2005, Miyazato played a tournament on the same circuit when it arrived in her home province. Unlike Wie, Miyazato didn't want to play against men, but her father accepted an invitation for her. Ai teed off in a lash of wind and rain—and finished last. "It was a local promotion," Miyazato explains. "I was trying to help."

Wie tore out ahead of Miyazato and most of the rest of the field, hitting every fairway and every green on the front nine. She birdied three on that side to put herself near the top of the leaderboard, where she would stay all week.

Wie charged like a horse that had been kept in the gate too long. And so did B.J. Wie. Even after tap-in par putts, he whooped much louder than usual. At one point, Michelle turned to Johnston and said, "He's embarrassing me."

Michelle didn't cool down. She birdied three more on the back to card a 6-under for the round. No 3-putts, no bogies. It was one of her best rounds of the year, and only Lorena Ochoa and her unconscious 10-under would lead Wie into Friday. After the round, Wie said she was "really hyped up." Miyazato called Wie "a perfect type of hero."

The only sign of trouble came in Wie's press conference interview, where she rolled her left wrist while she held the microphone in her right hand. The ailment was so obvious that a reporter asked about it. Wie admitted the injury for the first time publicly but said little else. Her wrist was obviously not slowing her down.

Not yet.

The next day didn't go as well. Wie's tee time wasn't until the afternoon, so she spent the time doing math homework and reading *The Great Gatsby*. That afternoon, she didn't look quite as pumped up. Her irons didn't leave her many birdie opportunities; she needed 34 putts. And yet she finished 1-under on the day.

Saturday was more of the same. She stumbled into the clubhouse at 1-over for the day and 6-under for the tournament. But the rest of the field was also drifting. The greens had hardened and nerves had softened. Ochoa still held the lead after the third round at 9-under, but she didn't seem sure of the ending. "In a major," she said, "you don't know what's going to happen."

Despite her so-so round, Wie seemed confident. She would be playing with Ochoa in the last pairing on Sunday. Asked if she felt pressure playing in the last group on a Sunday at a major—a fair question, considering how she'd struggled the summer before at the U.S. Women's Open—Wie said, "I tried to force things at the Open. If I'm destined to win, it's gonna happen. If not, I'm not."

Wie sounded calm, serene. Good thing, because the next day would be anything but.

The final group on Sunday showcased the LPGA's fondest dreams about combining entertainment and sports.

Ochoa has a doll's face. Shy but earnest, she speaks in a soft voice that makes her accented English seem truly heartfelt. She's candid: when asked if she supported drug testing on the Tour, Ochoa said, "I don't care. If someone else takes steroids, then I can take steroids, too." Despite a tiny frame, she's one of the biggest hitters on the tour. Not as long as Wie, but plenty long.

The two bombers would play with a bombshell, Natalie Gulbis, third going into Sunday at 4-under. At the time, Gulbis was still known more for her swimsuit calendar than her golf, but she had game as well. Tiger Woods' former coach, Butch Harmon, had helped her with an awkward swing and she willed herself closer and closer to a win. Her total package would make her the centerpiece of an *Esquire* magazine article later in the year, a rare feat for an LPGA player. Now, on the final day of the 2006 season's first major, she was playing in the final group for the championship.

The group had enough to interest everyone from wheezing hackers to frat boys, from teenage girls to Corona-swilling hombres from Guadalajara. All of the above showed up in Rancho Mirage on a cloudless Sunday.

And all of the above got an unforgettable show.

Wie came roaring out of her two-day hibernation with two birdies to close the gap to 2. She ate up the moment, tearing into every shot and chatting happily in between. Wie obviously loved the chase from close behind.

She came to the 9th with every club clicking. On the 508-

yard par 5, she dropped her third shot behind the pin and watched as Ochoa bogeyed. Wie then rolled in a slippery 10-footer to tie. She pumped a fist and practically ran to the 10th tee. The ovation from the packed gallery followed her, rattling across the nearby practice green, through the concession area, even into the clubhouse.

Nine holes to play for her first victory in a major, her first victory as a pro, her first victory of any kind since the 2003 U.S. Publinx.

Michelle Wie versus Lorena Ochoa: a two-horse race.

Or so it seemed.

Both parred 10 and 11, and then both got jittery. Wie's hips fired too early, and she blocked her drive on the 12th into the right rough. Ochoa did the same thing. Wie badly pulled a 7-iron trying to escape but still managed to make the green in two. Ochoa burned a hybrid along the grass, barely making it to the apron.

Advantage Wie? Not for long. She FedExed a 65-foot putt 15 feet by the hole and missed the comebacker. Bogey. Ochoa chipped up and two-putted. Bogey.

Still tied.

But Ochoa looked like she was breaking down. On 13, she spun out of another drive and pushed it into the right rough. She came short of the green, chipped up short of the hole again, and two-putted again for another bogey.

Wie split the fairway, made the green with ease, and faced a 10-footer for birdie that would mean a two-stroke swing.

B.J. Wie, usually right up against the rope with fists clenched, now stood well away from the green, under the shade of a solitary tree. He stared down into the grass. He slowly stepped out from under the tree and sidled to the green. His daughter stepped to her putt and knocked it close, then tapped it in for par.

Michelle was all alone in the lead. History was now hers to

lose—or so it seemed for a while. But the buzz along the ropes wasn't about Wie taking over as Ochoa faltered. The buzz came from up ahead, where Karrie Webb was making a charge.

Webb, then 31, had one of the most illustrious records in women's golf, with 6 majors and 29 other LPGA trophies on her mantelpiece to that point. The previous year, when she'd been inducted into the Hall of Fame, was her first without a victory since she joined the Tour in 1996. The day before, playing with the painfully slow Ochoa, had been a "bad mental day," she said afterward. But on Sunday morning, she read in the paper that Sorenstam, nine strokes off the lead, had said that she thought she still had a shot. Webb, only seven shots back, thought to herself, "Why not me?"

Hours later, with Ochoa drowning and Wie treading water, Webb was hydroplaning toward the clubhouse. And suddenly, after quietly following the leaders all day, Gulbis was in the mix, with a birdie on 13 to come within 2. From then on, every hole would feel like sudden death for the final threesome. The faces of Wie and Ochoa and Gulbis, so bright and perky on the first tee, now glistened with fatigue.

At the par-3 14th, Ochoa and Gulbis both found the green, while Michelle landed in a bunker. She blasted out to 15 feet and missed her par putt. Just like that, she, Ochoa, and Webb were all tied on top of the leaderboard at 7-under.

On the 16th hole, a 390-yard par 4, Wie blistered a perfect 5-wood to the middle of the fairway, then walked to the ball and folded her arms. She was both tense and excited. She whipped out a 7-iron and punched it right at the flag. Gimme. She waved to acknowledge the cheers from around the green and casually leaned on her club.

Wie tapped in for birdie, thinking it gave her the outright lead at 8 under with two holes to play. But then Johnston turned to her and said, "Just so you know, Karrie Webb eagled 18." Wie's eyes flew wide open. She was the outright leader, but only of her group: Webb, in the clubhouse at 9 under, was the leader of the tournament.

Wie had plenty of energy now. Too much. She overshot the flag on the par-3 17th by 40 feet. As she made her way toward the green, a fan yelled, "Watch out, Tiger! Here comes Michelle Wie!" She nestled a long lag close and made par. Standing on the green, Wie turned to Gulbis while Ochoa was lining up her putt and whispered, "Can you believe Karrie made eagle?" Ochoa made par to stay at minus-7. Then Gulbis sank a birdie putt to join Michelle in a tie for second behind Webb at 8 under.

One hole to play.

Wie and Gulbis needed birdies on the par-5 18th to force a play-off with Webb. Ochoa needed an eagle. Fans sprinted to the final tee. "Go Michelle!" yelled a little girl. Only 525 yards left.

Wie crushed the longest drive she'd had all week, leaving her only about 200 yards from the green. Thirty yards behind Michelle, Ochoa put everything in her small body into a 3-wood. It was a prayer, but she had no choice. A huge yelp went up from the stands. She'd landed on the green. Ochoa had a putt for eagle and a play-off.

Wie paid little mind. She knew an eagle would win her the championship. She had always hit an extra club length in big situations, and this was the biggest. She didn't even talk to Johnston about the decision. There was no decision. She scorched a 5-iron—yes, a *5-iron*—200 yards and through the green. Too much club? (Hard to imagine.) Too much adrenaline? (Likely.) Whatever, another roar went up around the green, so she still had a shot.

Gulbis laid up, pitched on—and missed her birdie putt. Goodbye, Natalie.

Wie had a choice to make. She was 25 feet away from the hole but sitting on the fringe. Chip? Or putt? Behind the ropes, B.J. thought putt. So did Johnston. But Wie was in control now, and Wie loved drama. She asked for a wedge. Again, there was no discussion.

One of the most famous shots in golf history had taken place just the year before at the 2005 Masters when Tiger Woods chipped in from the fringe on the 16th green. Woods had about 15 more feet and a much slicker green, but the idea was the same: get it on and rolling as quickly as possible. As any golf fan knows, his ball trickled along for what seemed like hours before dropping into the hole. Two holes later, he was in a play-off with Chris DiMarco. One hole after that, he slipped on his fourth green jacket.

Wie didn't chip like Tiger. Not just "not as well as"— nobody does—but also differently. She put more loft on the ball. This was no exception: her chip almost made it to the hole on the fly—and rolled 10 feet past.

Ochoa stared down her 8-foot eagle putt. Her eyes grew wide. The ball left her putter head, rolled straight and true, and dropped for eagle. Lorena Ochoa had collapsed and rebuilt herself in an hour. Hello, play-off.

Wie stepped to her ball. She read a slight left-to-right break. She hit it exactly where she wanted. The ball curved exactly where she wanted it to and rolled toward the hole, which looked ready to swallow it. Wie crouched down in hope, poised to leap up in triumph.

It lipped out.

Wie bent over at the waist, her head tucked down between her arms, her putter held aloft, for what seemed like an eternity. Finally she stood up, walked to the ball, and finished off her par.

Wie fans flipped out. Why not a nice lag putt from the fringe to set up a one-putt birdie? Why the much riskier shot with a wedge? A putt would have had every bit as much chance of dropping as the wedge, maybe more, and was a lot safer. It made no sense, not then and not now.

Old friend Tommy Kim, watching from Las Vegas, screamed at the television when he saw an iron in Wie's hand: *What are you doing?*

"She's not going to hole out for eagle," Kim said afterward. "Why not take your chances in a play-off? She made up her mind to win the tournament. Why? The only thing you can say is that she had some serious balls."

Kim wasn't the only one watching. Final-round viewership jumped 97 percent from the year before, when Wie finished in a tie for 14th. This time, Wie wanted to finish her first professional major with a Tiger-like moment. Asked after the round what she was thinking, Wie said she chipped "because it gave me the best chance to win."

But Wie critics had reason to boast once again that this young girl simply didn't know how to finish a tournament.

Karrie Webb won the play-off with Ochoa on the first hole. In the press tent afterward, she called the eagle on the 72nd hole the greatest moment of her Hall of Fame career.

But the buzz, as always, was around Michelle Wie. She wasn't just 16 and contending; she was 16 and on the verge of triumph. She had held her own against the LPGA's next great star, Lorena Ochoa; its next great starlet, Natalie Gulbis; and one of its all-time superstars, Karrie Webb.

Yes, she had lost in her characteristic, all-or-nothing daredevil style. And yes, many thought that the 16-year-old rising star had her comeuppance coming. Many predicted that Wie would someday have to pay a price for her iconoclasm, her impatience, and her confidence.

Maybe so.

But on this bright afternoon in the desert, when it took two final-hole eagles to beat her, it didn't seem like anything could stop her march to greatness.

The Kindest Cut

The main terminal at Seoul's Incheon Airport on Saturday, April 11, 2006, was jam-packed with photographers, reporters, TV crews, security guards, and a
hundred or so people there to meet someone. Not a relative coming back from a trip abroad, but a family member nonetheless.

Michelle Wie.

By her 1:30 ETA, the waiting area around terminal E was
wall-to-wall people. A half hour went by, then an hour. The
journalists went outside to smoke. A girl with flowers yawned.
A few fans left; many more sat on the floor despondently. When
was she going to get here?

Waiting for Wie was an appropriate symbol: the week
ahead would be her eighth attempt to make a cut in a men's
tournament. How long was *that* going to take? Finally, at 3:06
p.m., the doors from the runway swung open, and no one in
the terminal remembered the delay.

Michelle Wie wore Dolce & Gabbana wedges, an ivory

jacket and skirt, and a light blue blouse. Her hair was wavy, with brown highlights. She looked about 6'5" as she strode into the immense hallway like a politician on the campaign trail, smiling and waving. She accepted the bouquet from the little girl, smiled for another photo op, and gracefully made a beeline toward an escalator with a flock of cameras recording her every step.

Wie wasn't the first Korean American woman golfer to arrive in Seoul to great fanfare. Christina Kim burst onto the LPGA Tour and got an invite to play for South Korea against Japan in the Pinx Cup. She flew to the country of her parents' birth and ascended a dais to meet the Korean press. But Kim had no idea how seriously her parents' native country took both national pride and the game of golf. A few reporters began shouting at her, asking how a Korean American could justify taking such a prestigious spot from a South Korean. Kim broke into tears in front of the nation's gathered media.

Wie faced even more scrutiny. The South Koreans wanted to claim her as their own, but could they? "She's intensely popular," said Rick Phillips of the Korean Cultural Center of Los Angeles. "They are extremely proud of her. But that means she has a lot of pressure on her."

After a few minutes decompressing in a VIP lounge, Wie led the throng to a nearby room for a press conference, where she sat and smiled and held court, speaking in Korean. For the next week, she would be known in media sessions and at tee boxes and even on leaderboards not as Michelle or Big Wiesy, but as Wie Sung-mi, her given Korean name. And Wie Sung-mi spoke Korean at least as well as Michelle spoke English. Maybe better.

After the press conference, she and her parents ducked into cars and took off for Seoul. Waiting downtown, along with even more cameramen and reporters, were officials from SK

Telecom, the sponsors of the week's tournament. The Wies stopped briefly in a VP's office and then took an elevator downstairs to the basement, where some special fans waited in a lounge.

They were children. Not the adoring, giggly children who would line the galleries later in the week, but seriously sick children. One had no arms, and shook Michelle's hand with his feet. Another simply lay limp in her mother's arms as Michelle came over and compressed her long figure into a squat to look the small child in the eyes.

These kids needed surgery or treatment they couldn't afford. Wie had found out about their stories through B.J.'s brother-in-law, Heong, who was a pathologist in Korea. Heong stood in the room next to Bo and B.J. as Michelle handed out gifts from Nike and Sony. Besides smiles and hugs, Michelle gave $300,000, making her charitable donations for the year $800,000, which would surpass her year-end winnings. Her sadness was palpable. It was the most difficult moment of the whole visit.

Sky 72 Golf Club is a beautiful place in an ugly place, only recently carved out of a barren, rocky mountaintop, with the winding road to the clubhouse still strewn with enormous concrete slabs and other construction debris. And yet its vistas are majestic, with Seoul in the distance on one side and the sea in the distance on another. The hills are steep and the undulating fairways are crossed with rocky paths and meandering streams. The bracing wind makes sweaters near obligatory articles of dress.

But the course's most distinguishing feature is its greens: Sky 72 is one of only two courses in the nation with bentgrass greens. The wind, the hills, and the length—7,111 yards from the tips, featuring long par 3s and a 635-yard par 5—make it a stiff challenge, but the greens made it feel playable to a sixteen-year-old pro from America. Unlike in Japan, where a 3-foot putt lied to her eyes, Wie could score here.

She took to the course early Sunday, with Bo raking sand traps behind her and B.J. using his slope-measuring device and furiously scribbling in his notebook. Course officials served steaming bowls of *udon* to the Wies in a shelter after the 11th hole, with red bean pastries for dessert. The course's designer even went out with the Wies during a practice round and answered B.J.'s questions along the way.

The course played long, eternal compared to the compact Kraft Nabisco layout from a month before, but still Wie could use an occasional 5-wood off the tee. She played a relaxed practice round, as if she were back home on Ko Olina. Pressure only seemed to show up at lunch, and that had nothing to do with golf.

Michelle sat at the middle of a long table in a private room in the auxiliary clubhouse, her parents at her side and William Morris and Nike reps at the edges. Dozens of dishes were carted in. Wie ate and grinned and ate until she finally put her hands on her stomach and joked that she could feel herself bulging. And when the plates all but completely covered the table, Michelle put her face in her hands.

"I'm so nervous," she murmured.

The tournament? No. The baseball game. A local professional team had invited her to take a ceremonial first swing at an afternoon game. She'd spent more time on the course thinking about that swing than any other.

But this was Michelle Wie, so she was prepared. She knew the exact distance from the mound to home plate—60'6". At

Deborah Booker

When Michelle Wie was 10 years old, she could hit a golf ball 300 yards. That's not a typo—300 yards. Her favorite golfer was Tiger Woods. Her goal was to beat him…"in the near future."

Team Wie: Michelle's parents, Bo and B.J., who have seen virtually every golf swing their daughter has made as a junior, amateur, and pro.

At age 13, Michelle won the 2003 USGA Women's Amateur Public Links Championship—the youngest person in USGA history to win an adult championship.

David Cannon / Getty Images

Robert Laberge / Getty Images

Teammates on the victorious American team at the 2004 Curtis Cup matches in England, Wie and Paula Creamer went head-to-head in the second round of the 2005 Kraft Nabisco Championship.

Steve Grayson / WireImage

Donald Miralle / Getty Images

The Big Easy and the Big Wiesy hit it off from the minute they first played together in the Pro-Am before the 2004 Sony Open, a PGA Tour stop in Hawaii, so much so that they part-nered up a year later at the same event.

Sarah Friedman / Corbis

Dressed for success for a feature in Fortune *(2005). Suit and shirt by Escada. Styling by Kiersten Large. Hair and makeup by Elena Arroy for Vincent Longo. Attitude by Wie.*

Drive for show, putt for dough. *It's a cliché for a reason. If Michelle had been just an average putter, she'd have won at least one major, probably two, by now on the LPGA Tour. If she can get a grip on the flat stick, she still might live up to the impossibly high expectations that have tracked her since she told David Letterman in 2005 of her ambition to play in the Masters.*

Lisa Blumenfeld / Getty Images

Jeff Gross / Getty Images

Andrew Redington / Getty Images

Yes! *In December 2008, after two injury-plagued years and multiple disappointments, Michelle Wie earned her LPGA Tour card for the 2009 golf season with a strong showing at the Tour's Q-school. Does this fist pump mark the beginning of the Wie Era in women's golf?*

Scott Halleran / Getty Images

the ballpark she put on a full uniform with the number 54 on the back. Caddy Greg Johnston asked her why 54, and Wie gave him a smile. "You should know," she said. Then it dawned on him: 54 would be 18 under on a par-72 course, a birdie on every hole.

Michelle walked out to home plate, acknowledged a round of enthusiastic applause with a huge smile and wave, and stepped into the batter's box. She missed the first two pitches, then fouled two back, lined one back at the pitcher, and sprayed two into the outfield. As always, she was a quick learner.

That night, Wie appeared on a TV talk show in a flowing black dress, outdoors on a patio overlooking the Pacific, with a South Korean version of Katie Couric. Michelle laughed as an oddball in a baseball uniform did a string of jokes delivered on tape, and she made pleasant chit-chat with a South Korean TV heartthrob whom her mom watched religiously. She seemed more at ease than she had on *60 Minutes*. On CBS, Michelle talked about eventually having a family. On the South Korean station, she joked that her dream guy would be taller than she is and able to do housework.

But the lightest moment of the week came the next day, at a driving range almost large enough to be a course in itself. She was there to give a clinic—with camera crews there to record every minute, of course—to amateur golfers in search of tips. Michelle put a wireless microphone on and gave tips to players of all ages, from an elderly gentleman with a slice—"Don't rush your swing," she told him in Korean. "Keep the same tempo"— to a middle-aged woman looking for extra distance. Then, at the end of the line, up stepped a little girl.

The girl wobbled around with a driver that looked to be only a couple of feet long. She had pigtails, a dress, and tiny shoes. Her name was Seon Hwa Hong. She was 5.

Before swinging, Hong had a gift for Wie. So the six-footer

crouched low and waited. Hong, shy, first turned away, then began to sing. "Cheer Michelle Wie! Cheer Michelle Wie!" she sang in Korean, her voice high and bouncy. Everyone grinned and cooed. Michelle broke into an enormous grin.

After her song, Hong grabbed a club and addressed the ball. She began her backswing, the club winding around her body and looking like it might topple her. Then she spun back around, the dress swirling and the white tights a mini-blur, and swung through the ball. Wie let out a huge "Whoooooaaaa!" as the little girl's drive jumped, soared more than 75 yards, and bounced almost to the 100-yard sign. Everyone cheered. B.J. said that it brought back memories of his own daughter on that baseball field in Oahu when she was four.

Only later did Michelle and her parents learn about the huge white van out in the parking lot with a yellow banner draped on the side, with a bigger-than-life-size picture of Seon Hwa Hong, age five, putting with a Yes brand C-groove putter. The little girl had a sponsor. She also had a nickname: "Michelle."

Wie was treated like a beloved member of the family in South Korea. On the course and on the practice range, she was greeted with shouts of "Big sister!" Back home in Hawaii there were plenty of detractors who'd become sick of all the hype and felt she'd gotten too big for the little state that could. Not in Seoul. The media referred to her as a Korean playing in the United States, instead of an American visiting South Korea.

"Michelle Wie is a great blessing for Koreans," said Michael Won of *Korea Daily,* an English-language newspaper published in Seoul as well as America. "We never had such a successful figure worldwide. Nobody has ever paid such attention to a Korean like this."

Michelle returned the love. She looked much more like a girl coming home to visit friends and family than a celebrity dealing with the pressure of a professional golf tournament, the barrage of demands from the media, and the fatigue of an eighteen-hour time zone switch. This was a different Michelle Wie—more worldly, more charismatic, more composed, more comfortable—than had been seen back home in a long time.

The 2006 SK Telecom Open was originally to have been a virtual homecoming celebration for K.J. Choi, who had won the event in 2005 and was returning to defend his title. The big-shouldered 26-year-old had three PGA Tour wins under his belt at the time and was well on his way to becoming what he is today, the most internationally successful Asian golfer of all time, masculine division. Then Michelle Wie signed on, and suddenly the rising PGA Tour star had to share the marquee with a 16-year-old girl. And there were plenty of signs he wasn't delighted about it.

Back in January, at the Sony Open, Choi said that Wie shouldn't make a habit of playing in PGA Tour events until she went to the LPGA's Q-School and won her card. Now, at the SK Telecom, he scheduled his press conference immediately after Wie's, and swooped in as she was finishing to stand for a photo op with the taller girl. He got up onto his tiptoes for a laugh, and then pressed down on Wie's shoulder for another. He complimented Wie for her "nerves," smiling broadly all the while.

But newspapers reported that Choi declined a tournament official's request to pair with Wie, and two sources said he refused to share a press conference with her. Choi knew that this year MBC, the Korean broadcasting station, had paid to cover the tournament; previously, the SK Telecom had paid the Korean TV network to secure coverage. The difference, of course, was Michelle Wie.

Founded in 2004, the Asian Tour was a de facto minor league for the PGA Tour, with Asian, Australian, and American players honing their games, hoping to make the jump across the Pacific. The Asian Tour's likely future didn't look minor at all: if golf spreads to China and India—and few doubt that it will, someday—the Asian Tour could well grow into a very major league.

"We all knew when Tiger hit the scene that he would be special." Louis Martin, a South African who was CEO of the Asian Tour at that time, was explaining the SK Telecom sponsor's decision to extend Michelle Wie an invitation to play in their tournament. "She's the same thing. She will bring people who are not golf-oriented to golf."

And what about the fact that she had turned pro less than seven months earlier, that she hadn't yet won a pro tournament? "How could people expect that? I've heard her compared to Anna Kournikova. She will do it all."

Shouldn't she play with women only? "I don't want to criticize the LPGA. I know they don't want to bend the rules. But it's a positive she's not on that tour, because it gives us a chance."

Wasn't she costing someone a spot? "I don't accept that. Invitees are exactly that. Sometimes it's a mother's brother's son. There are special cases. And no one can argue that."

Why didn't more people agree? "I think it's jealousy. People wonder how she can command all that money. 'What has she done?' But . . . how do you define charisma? She's got something. There really is no reason for anyone to be negative at all."

So she wasn't overhyped? "She's the best thing that's happened in golf since Tiger."

Then what was next for her? "No doubt she'll rewrite the books. She's the full package."

Hak Lee, vice president of the Korean PGA and chairman of the Asian Tour rules committee, agreed with Martin that

Michelle Wie was something special, but he didn't agree that she should be playing in the SK Telecom: "I think the men's tour should be played by men. She should be a star player in the future. Right now she's just a little girl."

Could she make the cut? "So far, she has failed. It would be a sensation if she does it, but I don't think it will help the Asian Tour at all. People will question the quality of the tour, and that I don't like."

What had this experience been like for him? "MBC invested $3 million. They asked me to give her the 11:10 a.m. tee time on Friday. But the first priority goes to K.J. Choi. This is not a spotlight for Michelle Wie only. . . . There will be a lot of spectators, and I don't know if the marshals can control them or not."

And was it worth it? "This could depress her. There is so much pressure. If she doesn't make it, it could change her game."

Hundreds of fans packed around the tee box on the 10th hole. Others stood on rocks, stone fences, and even the clubhouse rooftop. They were there to see Michelle Wie hit her first drive in the 2006 SK Telecom Open.

It was 6:59 a.m.

Wearing an orange zip-up, Wie pushed her way through the adoring mob to get to the first tee. Greg Johnston, more accustomed to the decorum and relative serenity of an LPGA Tour event, looked frustrated already. Unlike at a tournament back home, with officials at the ropes standing by to admonish camera-phone users, no marshals at the SK Telecom made a peep about the technology in the gallery. So the *click-click-click* started as soon as Wie emerged from the crowd to tee up her ball, and it didn't stop even when she stepped away from her address because of all the clatter.

The first hole—a 546-yard par 5—set the tone for the entire tournament. She bombed a drive longer than one of her male playing partners, followed with a fairway wood to wedge range, had to step away from her ball again because of all the commotion and clicking, and still stuck her approach to within 12 feet of the pin.

Then came the real drama. Wie's putting had killed her in Japan. Would this be any different? She had a test to start: a quick downhill roll.

Wie stood tall over the ball. She eyed the line and, at the last second before striking, she leaned slightly onto her front foot. The move gave her a visible stability. She stroked the ball with authority, and it rolled straight into the hole. Birdie.

Wie had a new ally. David Leadbetter's wife, Kelly, had won the Women's Amateur Public Links title in 1977 and 1978—the same tournament Michelle Wie won in 2003—before joining the LPGA Tour in 1981, where she played on and off for 17 years. She never won a Tour event, but she carved out a decent reputation as a clutch putter. So her husband introduced her to Michelle.

Kelly Leadbetter noticed right away that Wie looked "bunched" over the ball. Her height, so much of a gift in her long game, was a curse on the greens. Leadbetter straightened Wie's spine, moved her closer to the ball, and instructed Wie to make up her mind firmly and absolutely before taking the putter back. That didn't address Wie's main putting problem, reading slope and distance, but on this day, Wie appeared calm and unhurried. She one-putted eight holes and three-putted none.

The constant noise of shuffling feet and rifling apertures obviously wore on Johnston and Wie's playing partners. But Wie smiled and chatted as much as she had all season. She stepped away from her ball when necessary, but each post-interruption shot was flawless. And instead of making a bee-line for her ball and leaving the others in her wake—the old Wie—she lagged and chatted about how she felt *The 40-Year-Old Virgin* was too much of a guy movie but *Star Wars* was fun to watch.

Wie finished the first day at 2-under, good for a tie for 28th. A couple of hours after she holed out on the ninth, a Kansas City pro named Clay Devers sat in the lobby of the players' hotel in Seoul. He'd withdrawn from the tournament with a broken toe, but stuck around to cheer on friends and work on his putting. When the players' bus pulled in, he greeted a buddy with a smile:

"So how's it feel to be beaten by a sixteen-year-old girl?"

Friday was a holiday in South Korea: Children's Day. Galleries that numbered in the hundreds on Thursday swelled to thousands on cut day. Perfect weather coupled with no school brought out such large crowds that fans flooded onto the course without a ticket.

To add to the carnival atmosphere of Children's Day, tournament officials hired a "K.J. Choi" and a "Michelle Wie" for the day. And there they were, standing side-by-side on the grounds just outside the clubhouse, a short, brawny Korean man in a Nike cap next to a tall, leggy Korean woman in a Nike bucket hat and chandelier earrings. They smiled and waved and posed for pictures as people made their way from the parking lot onto the course. From a distance, the woman might have passed for Wie, even though she was 12 years older.

One minor inconsistency: the woman's golf dress was a bit shorter than anything Michelle would ever wear. In the club-house, the faux Michelle bent over to tie her Nike shoe and inadvertently revealed a little too much to a group of onlookers. Officials had to usher her into a private room to tell her to be more careful.

The real Michelle Wie wore pants, though from the time she left the clubhouse to make her way to the practice range she was so engulfed by a crush of fans that all you could see of her wardrobe was her Nike bucket hat. Even the practice green had a five-deep gallery. When Wie finally got to the first tee, she looked around and appeared a bit stunned by the mammoth crowd.

Golf Nation waited expectantly. Another missed cut at a men's event could be devastating to a season that had taken off with her third-place finish at the Kraft Nabisco. Wie's next two scheduled attempts at men's tournaments would be on the PGA Tour, with much stiffer competition than she faced in the SK Telecom. The weather was good, the course was playable, the greens were familiar, the galleries were behind her, and she was coming off a strong first round.

If not now, when?

Now.

After seven futile attempts in four years, Michelle Wie had fulfilled a promise to herself to prove that she had what it took—talent, temperament, balls—to compete with men in a game that she'd been playing for a dozen years.

She looked happy enough in her post-round interview on Korean TV but admitted to being "very frustrated" with her final round, a 74 in the rain-shortened 54-hole tournament that left her tied for 35th. Her usually strong iron play, superlative on Thursday and Friday, let her down on Sunday, leaving her too many long, difficult putts. And putting was still her weakest suit, by far.

To Michelle Wie fans everywhere, her final finish was irrelevant. This was the week when she finally broke through to become only the third woman in history to make a cut in a men's professional golf tournament. It was a moment to be savored until her next giant step up the ladder to golf immortality. And that step might come soon: she had been accepted as only the second woman ever to play a European Tour event, the Omega Masters in September.

But by no means was everybody in Golf Nation a Wie fan, leastways not anymore. The novelty had worn off. She was no longer the brash 14-year-old who'd charmed top PGA Tour pros back in 2004 at the Sony Open in Hawaii. She was now a big-time marketing machine, a multimillion-dollar brand, but still just a teenager who hadn't made her bones in the game, much less dominated it.

Making the cut in South Korea didn't soften the criticism. She still hadn't won anything, critics noted, and making the cut at the SK Telecom said more about the quality of golf on the Asian Tour than about Wie's ability to compete with top male pros.

A commentator on the Canadian Web site Sportsnet.ca named John Gordon pretty much summed up the anti-Wie feeling:

> Are you as sick as me, and just about everyone else I talk to, of hearing about Michelle Wie? So she finally found a men's tour in South Korea where she could make the cut after seven failed attempts on the PGA, Nationwide, and Canadian tours. Big deal. She's just 16, so she'll have lots of time to attempt to become the first woman to make a PGA Tour cut since Babe Didrikson Zaharias did it in Tucson in 1945, after she proves she can win on the LPGA. Makes you wonder what her motivation is.

Another blogger chimed in: "Isn't her 15 minutes of fame used up yet?"

And another: "I was sick of hearing about her the second time she was mentioned, to be honest. Are her parents pushing her for her sake, or for their pocketbooks? I don't think we'll ever really know."

And . . . well, you get the picture.

Then there was Charlie Wi, a Korean-born Asian Tour player who'd starred at the University of California. He finished only one stroke ahead of Wie at the SK Telecom but still told the *San Jose Mercury News,* "I don't think she belongs out there" and "I don't think we want that kind of circus every week."

The Wies didn't care. They continued to build up Michelle's endorsement portfolio at a relentless clip; they stayed in South Korea for a Nike appearance and to put the final touches on a deal with a real estate company. In return for a few commercial shoots in New York and Hawaii over the summer, Michelle would earn $3 million. Basis for comparison? The year before, Annika Sorenstam had topped the LPGA money list with $2,588,240, just over $1 million more than number two on the money list, Paula Creamer.

The money rolled in, but so did the appointments and the appearances. Could Wie chew everything she bit off? So far, the only yellow flag was the occasional flare-up with her left wrist, but that hadn't hindered her game at all. (Key words: "so far.") To all appearances, Michelle Wie was happy, successful, and still on the way up.

But now came the end of the school year, the beginning of a long stretch away from home, and the most demanding time of Michelle Wie's life.

This Close

There was something noticeably different in the air.

B.J. and Bo Wie walked down the 11th fairway of the Canoe Brook Country Club North Course in Summit, New Jersey, just west of Manhattan. They were smiling broadly. Michelle, trailing behind during a practice round before the biggest day of her life, stared straight ahead. Wie Sung-mi had stayed behind in South Korea, and Michelle Wie was back, intense as ever. Two reporters followed close by; she paid them no mind. A deer ran through the nearby trees; she paid it no mind. She smiled little and said less all day.

The next morning, TV trailers would line up by the range and a concession hut would be remade into an ESPN studio. The Mall at Short Hills next door would reserve a thousand parking spots. An old used-car lot half a mile from the course would provide media parking and shuttle service. And the media credentials printed for the next day (160) would outnumber those for the players on the course (153).

Big-money stop on the PGA Tour? No, a sectional qualifying tournament for the 2006 United States Open.

But on this sleepy summer Monday in early June a 16-year-old girl was going to play 36 holes of golf. If she played well enough, she would become a golf legend.

No woman had ever qualified to play in the U.S. Open—the men's version—or any other men's major golf tournament. In fact, no woman had ever emerged from local qualifying for the U.S. Open. Wie tackled that stage in Honolulu only a week after returning from making the cut in the SK Telecom in South Korea. She had to score low enough on 18 holes to win one of three slots open to a field of 40 men and, of course, one girl.

She finished first.

"Awesome," Wie replied to the USGA official who brought her the news.

The first woman in history to advance to sectional qualifying would play her next round here in Summit, New Jersey, against the likes of Mark O'Meara, Bernhard Langer, and about 200 other male golfers, professionals and amateurs. Roughly 20 golfers would then go on to play in the 2006 U.S. Open later that summer at Winged Foot Golf Club in Mamaroneck, New York, one of the most storied tracks in the world of golf.

Why New Jersey? Michelle could have stayed in Hawaii and played in the sectional qualifier there, with all the local love and less of the national competition. Instead, the Wies flew first to northern Maryland, site of the LPGA Championship, scheduled to begin only three days after the Open sectionals, so Michelle could practice. They then drove in a rented minivan to New Jersey.

The decision made no sense. Why practice on a women's

course, with greens cut at one length, then play on a men's course, with another cut, then return to the first course? Once Wie got one putting speed down, it would be time to switch to another speed, and then back again. But the Wie ambition knew no limits. It was the way the family thought. When facing a choice between A and B, they invariably opted for C.

Leading up to sectionals, *Sports Illustrated* ran a first-person column by Rick Hartmann, the jovial head pro from a club on Long Island who was slated to play in Wie's group. The headline: "Why Me? Help! I'm Playing with Michelle Wie in a U.S. Open Qualifier." *USA Today*'s Ian O'Connor reported on Jack Nicklaus' "100 percent" support of Wie's effort if she qualified. Reports from Europe rang in with defending U.S. Open champ Michael Campbell's comment that "she's got to prove that she can win on the women's tour before she can even have a chance on the men's tour." Gambling sites such as Gambling911.com and PinnacleSports.com offered action on whether Wie would make it, putting her odds at slightly better than 7 to 1 against.

"The national media will descend on Canoe Brook Country Club in Summit like locusts," wrote Stephen Edelson of the *Asbury Park Press*. "The normally subdued event known as U.S. Open sectional qualifying will be turned into nothing short of a circus sideshow thanks to her presence."

*Side*show? No, Wie's presence made it the main event. One day after Wie made sectionals, USGA media relations director Craig Smith fielded an e-mail from a reporter asking about credentials for Canoe Brook. "None needed," Smith wrote back, "just show up and join the party."

But at any really good party, the room fills up a little faster than the party throwers expect. Sectionals were normally quiet enough for the few gallery members to hear conversations between players and caddies; now the USGA had a rock concert on its hands.

Wie played in a group with Hartmann and David Gossett, a winner of the U.S. Amateur and the John Deere Classic. Organizers, knowing Wie would create enough stir to clog the entire course, decided to put her group last, at 8:35 a.m., off the easier South Course and then at 2:20 p.m., off the more difficult North Course. The 36-hole odyssey would take 11 hours.

The day would not feel long.

Wie laughed as she arrived at the course just after dawn, stunned and yet touched to see so many media and fans waiting for her. She went through her normal pre-round routine, putting as Bo held her head steady, while dozens of reporters recorded every movement she made.

More than a thousand spectators lined up for the first shot of Wie's day. Crowd control would be a problem all day. More than 6,000 fans flooded the premises, so many that the course had to close the entrance at 11:00 a.m. Even that didn't keep people out. The qualifier didn't have gallery ropes—none had ever been needed before—so reporters and fans walked on the fairway, sometimes within arm's length of the players.

The fixation on Wie was such that spectators walked next to Gossett and Hartmann, oblivious to them or their upcoming shots. The two other pros almost disappeared into the crowd, like just another couple of guys in golf gear out to watch Wie. Gossett, after badly hooking his first shot, walked up the fairway laughing at the scene. Even Wie's two accompanying security guards, both from the Summit (N.J.) Police Detective Bureau (and both carrying handcuffs and guns), got lost in the throng.

*Ooh*s and *aah*s tracked Michelle's tee shots; nothing new there. A tricky 10-footer to save par on the first; now *that* was something. Bo yelled her standard *"Yessss!"* The crowd burst into applause, and the mob moved on. Back in the snack-shack-cum-TV-studio, ESPN reporter Tom Rinaldi prepared for his first cut-in. The drama had just begun.

Wie took off her coral sweater on the next hole; things were heating up. On the third hole, she stared down a dogleg left around a large bunker. Gossett and Hartmann played it safe, using irons to knock it to the turn and no farther. Wie launched a 5-wood that seemed to be locked in on the bunker. She walked to the right of the tee box to coax her ball away from the sand, then let out a half laugh as it bounced safely on the other side.

But Canoe Brook found Wie's weakness, too. This was yet another men's course with slick greens and *Poa annua* grass rather than the Bermuda she was reared on in Hawaii. Wie had 10-footer after 10-footer, but a 10-footer on this course had as many twists as a 30-footer at the tournament she was coming off in South Korea. On the 4th, she knocked a gorgeous 7-iron over a bunker to within 4 feet, but she lipped out her putt and looked skyward in disbelief.

Wie came right back two holes later: 275-yard tee shot, 210-yard 5-wood over a trap to the fringe, good chip to 4 feet, birdie. Easy game when you play it right.

The crowd swelled. One man had a tiny periscope, which looked ripped from a bathtub-sized submarine, so he could look over the crowd at Wie. On the 11th, two college-age guys stood by the tee box as Wie took a practice cut.

"Pretty swing," said one.

"Pretty ass," offered the other.

The 15th brought another classic Wie moment. She pushed her drive on the long par 4 and landed in a divot. Wie claimed she could see standing water if she stood by the ball. Rules official Jim Litvack came over, looked down, and shook his head. Wie could only have relief if she could see the water at address. She couldn't. Wie glanced at Johnston and then smiled in frustration.

Wie took out her 5-wood. A 5-wood for a ball in a divot? Was she crazy? She swung and the ball rocketed toward the low-slung clouds and the green. It trickled on, and fans were almost too stunned to cheer. It was the shot of the day—so far. USGA rep Beth Murrison, working crowd control, turned away from the gallery to stare and shook her head in amazement. As Wie headed up the fairway, several spectators stayed behind to study the gash she'd left in the ground. They gawked at the divot as if a meteor had landed.

Behind shimmering sunglasses, Litvack smiled. "I felt like crap," he said of the ruling he'd had to make. "Then she hit a great ball. Now I don't feel like crap."

On the par-4 18th, Wie found her second shot on an elevated slope looking down at the green, 50 feet from the flag. Bogey was going to be a good score, considering the sharp incline she had to traverse. She took an ever-so-soft swing, but even so the ball skittered across the green. "*Sit! Sit!*" somebody cried. Fat chance. Then a low, uh-oh rumble turned into a low, expectant roar as the ball headed right at the flag. At near full speed, it plowed right into the yellow flagstick and vanished. A roar exploded and reverberated over the course. *Birdie!*

Wie bent over laughing and then practically skipped down the green to collect her ball. Fans rushed the scorer's tent, even though a no-autographs, no-interviews policy was in effect. A cart came to rescue her. On the long walk through a tunnel to the clubhouse, PR reps and civilians whipped out their Black-Berry units and cells to inform friends, as if they had just spotted Bruce Springsteen at the grocery store.

Michelle Wie, with a 2-under 68, was halfway to Winged Foot.

One word reverberated in the media center all through lunch: *she.* She was tied for 13th. No, she was tied for 8th. She would be out if the sectional ended right now. No, she would be in. A reporter called up PGATour.com, which had a big head on the home page: "Wie've Got You Covered!"

If Michelle Wie matched her performance on the first eighteen that afternoon, she would tee it up with Tiger and Vijay and Ernie at the U.S. Open.

She was preposterously close to something preposterous.

The Wie buzz, as palpable as the humidity, had never been higher, but it drowned the hard truth that she had missed six birdie chances from inside 12 feet. The look of confidence on the greens in South Korea, where she seemed to know exactly where the putt was going before she struck the ball, was gone.

"The whole deal for her was a mental thing," said Kelly Leadbetter, David's wife, who started working on Wie's putting stroke after Japan. "She wasn't committing. Be positive, commit, and let it happen."

But that was just it: Wie was all about *making* things happen. That's how she'd lived—and played—her entire life. Could she *let* anything happen? She came from two parents who planned everything down to the tiniest detail. Now it seemed one of the family's greatest strengths, their striving for perfection, was turning out to be a weakness.

Wie walked out to the North Course in the afternoon and started her second 18 on the par-4, 373-yard 10th. She immediately pulled her tee shot left into a bunker. She could only pitch out and make bogey, falling back to 1-under for the day. The cut looked to be 4-under. Those missed putts were looking larger and larger.

Wie fought on, making par after par after par. On the 17th, a 455-yard par 4 to a blind fairway, she blistered a drive straight out. She and Johnston walked toward the group of white dots in the growing haze and stopped at the first ball. Wie assumed hers was the shortest of the three drives; it wasn't. She slipped away from the first ball casually and walked toward her own. Catching on, the huge crowd laughed and cheered.

Next, as if for emphasis, she whipped out an iron and dropped her shot 10 feet from the cup. Another roar. And when she nailed her birdie putt, a third cheer rattled along the trees. She was back to 2-under with 10 holes left. Nineteen players were at 3-under or better. Maybe a single birdie would do the trick.

The afternoon heat rose, enveloping Wie like a shawl. Her face began to glisten. The marshals began to allow fans to swarm the fairway behind the group. She played on, locked in on the moment. She finished 30 holes at a sizzling 2-under. Veteran reporters agreed that they had never seen so young a person do so well under such circumstances. A *New York Times* photographer caught her ponytail at the top of her follow-through; that picture would go on the top of the front page of the next day's paper.

Wie arrived at the 4th tee, her 32nd hole of the day, and showed a barely perceptible sign of strain: her back, always ramrod straight, bent just slightly at her shoulders. Fatigue had crept in. She missed the fairway with a 3-wood. She hit a nice recovery shot over a ravine to within 25 feet, which she lagged to 3 feet. A row of fans crowned the fairway, gazing over the water hazard as she stepped up to her par putt. The collective gasp told the story: miss.

Wie pulled her cap lip down over her eyes. After a few long seconds, she tapped in for bogey.

Everybody—Bo and B.J., Johnston, the onlookers, even Michelle—realized in that instant that she was done. The crowd around her went so silent you could hear the faint rustle of leaves in the wind. Sure, she had five holes to go and three birdies would do, so technically she could still . . . No. She was done.

Bogey.

Bogey.

Par.

Par.

Par.

Michelle Wie walked off the course after the last par at plus 1, five strokes out of a play-off. Her putter had done her in again.

"I'm very proud of her," B.J. said afterward. "A little disappointed, but very proud. I think Michelle demonstrated that it's possible for a woman to play in a men's major."

Michelle shot back: "I think finally my dad said something right."

And one final thought: "Hopefully, this just shows or motivates people to do what they want to do. I feel a lot more motivated after today."

Team Wie left New Jersey that night and arrived at the Bulle Rock Country Club in Havre de Grace, Maryland, the next day. The rest of the field for the LPGA Championship had already scouted out the course and prepared for the second-biggest weekend of their season. But the biggest event of Wie's season had just happened.

She said she felt like she was "eighty years old."

14

Learning to Read

If there were ever a course built for Michelle Wie, it's the Bulle Rock golf club, in Havre de Grace, Maryland, a rolling 6,596-yard track with wide fairways, few fairway bunkers, and gentle rough. A true bomber's paradise.

That became clear on the second hole, a 555-yard par 5 that descended into a valley, past a forbidding stream, and up to an elevated green. Most LPGA Tour players wouldn't even think of trying to reach it in two. Michelle Wie did. She never gave *not* going for it a thought. But her second shot didn't quite get there and a poor chip rolled 25 feet past the hole, so two putts added up to par. Opportunity missed.

Her partner that first day, Dorothy Delasin, then in her seventh year on the Tour, took a different approach: a medium-distance drive that spotted Wie's a hundred yards, a nice layup, a nice pitch shot, a nice putt, birdie.

Wie missed a 6-footer for birdie on the 3rd hole and double-bogeyed the 5th with a blocked tee shot into the right rough, a poor approach that missed the green, a tentative chip that stayed on the fringe, and three putts, including a 4-footer.

Michelle's face sagged, and she walked off the green as if in a trance. The 36 holes she'd played three days before, trying to qualify for the men's U.S. Open, was obviously taking its toll.

B.J. Wie stared straight ahead, expressionless. He realized that his daughter was fried. Did he also realize that he was responsible?

The rest of the front nine was pretty much the same, save for a 20-foot birdie putt on 9 that elicited a halfhearted fist pump. She made the turn with a 1-over 37. The crowd that shuffled with her to the back nine, only a hundred or so in number, was her smallest of the year.

But Wie bounced back. She let go of some of the tension by talking to Delasin about movie stars they both thought were cute—Christian Bale, Hayden Christenson, Matthew McConaughey. ("I keep forgetting she's 16," Delasin, 25, said later. "But it was nice to talk about something non-golf-related.") Birdies on the final two holes got Wie to a 1-under 71, which put her seven shots off the lead.

Meeting the press afterward, she admitted having "fought through the round." After a little hole-by-hole, a reporter asked why she chose New Jersey for her U.S. Open qualifying attempt instead of Hawaii. "I'm not good at picking spots," Wie said, smiling. "I leave that up to my mom and dad." The reporter pursued it, informing her that a 15-year-old boy she beat in the local qualifier actually won the Hawaii sectional and earned a trip to Winged Foot by beating only nine other contestants.

Wie's eyes widened. She suddenly realized that she might have made history simply by staying home. "One out of *ten*?" she asked. "Can I have another chance?"

• • • • •

B.J. and Bo Wie now had made not one mistake but two.

If they'd simply stayed in Hawaii, Michelle would've had a much better shot at the U.S. Open. That was a difficult enough possibility to mull. But perhaps even more damaging was the trip from Hawaii to New Jersey before the trip to Maryland. The travel had sapped their daughter, as did the extra practice, robbing her of precious energy for the LPGA. Her putting had killed her in both places. Trouble reading greens? Absolutely. But couldn't exhaustion have also played a key role?

Team Wie's compound blunder triggered two related questions: What was Michelle Wie's top priority? More important, what was B.J. Wie's top priority?

If it was to play in the U.S. Open—one of Michelle's two biggest dreams since she started playing golf, along with playing in the Masters—then she should have stayed home and tried to qualify in Hawaii, where it would have been several orders of magnitude easier. But playing the sectional there on June 5 would then have required flying halfway across the globe to the LPGA, which began on June 8. That would have made no sense.

Was it to win the LPGA Championship, a tournament in which she'd finished second the year before? Then Wie should never have played 36 holes on Monday in Hawaii *or* New Jersey. Yes, Michelle could walk and chew gum at the same time, but trying to qualify for one major and playing in another *in the same week*?

Unless . . . unless B.J.'s number one priority for Michelle, after consulting with the William Morris Agency, was maximum exposure, which could translate into more endorsement money down the line.

B.J. didn't hear Michelle ask jokingly for "another chance" to qualify for the U.S. Open because he was too busy laying down the law to caddy Greg Johnston as the two stood on a hill near where Michelle took questions. B.J. said point-blank to the caddy: "Don't help her on the greens anymore." What? Johnston was her caddy; it's only the single most important part of a caddy's job to help his player read greens, especially a player who needed as much help as Michelle Wie.

And she got help, but from then on it came from her daddy exclusively. Before every tournament, B.J. Wie marched out to every green and filled a course book with arrows denoting the slope and direction of possible putts. Michelle carried the book in her back pocket during rounds and consulted it for just about everything but tap-ins.

"When I caddied for her," says Gary Gilchrist, "B.J. was there watching every single step. It's quite uncomfortable, because you don't want to make a mistake. He carries these binoculars that could see Mars. And he'd stand right behind her with them. Bottom line, Michelle is going to make mistakes, and the caddy will make mistakes, but she can still win a major."

Three birdies on the front nine and two more on the back—and only one bogey—added up to a 4-under 68 on Friday. Great score, considering that she missed three birdie putts from fewer than 5 feet.

As usual, she was the biggest hitter on the course, her iron play was solid, and her off-on chipping was more on than off. But her 5-under score after two days could have been 10-under without a flock of makeable putts that she didn't make. She admitted that she "left a lot of putts out there," and by now the press had caught on to Johnston's absence from her pre-putt prep. While she lined up putts, sometimes consulting B.J.'s notes, Johnston would be standing well away from her, not close at hand as did other caddies.

Even the best PGA Tour players use caddies for reads. Tiger Woods won his first PGA Championship at Medinah in 1999 in part because of a gutsy call by Steve Williams, who insisted a key 8-foot putt on the 71st hole was inside left when Tiger thought otherwise. (P.S.: Tiger made the putt. His margin of victory over Sergio Garcia was . . . one stroke.)

"She's not taking advantage of the advantage" is how one reporter put it after learning that Johnston had been relieved of green-reading duties. And that was strange, because B.J. was always looking for an edge; that's why he'd practically memorized the rule book. But then to deprive her of Johnston's proven expertise on the greens? It was as if his independent streak had short-circuited his competitive streak. B.J. explained to the press that week that Johnston would no longer be consulted because Michelle needed to learn to read greens "on her own."

Saturday brought more great shot-making and more missed putts. After a nice birdie on 1, Michelle made a nifty rescue from the trees on 2, but missed a 10-footer to save par. Then she three-putted 3 for another bogey. She birdied 4 with a 10-footer, then lipped out a 5-footer to give it back on 5.

On 16, facing a 6-footer to save par, she stepped to the edge of the green, looked back down the fairway, raised an index finger, and locked her eyes on it as she drew figure-eights in the air. This was a maneuver taught to her by her fitness trainer, Paul Gagné, who uses it to help with balance and equilibrium. Gagné believes the body often gets distorted, with one shoulder slightly lower than the other. Realigning vision with the figure-eights, he believes, helps realign posture.

She made the putt.

On 17, a 171-yard par 3, Wie launched a mid-iron to within 20 feet. Birdie time? Not so fast. She left her first putt 3 feet short. Her second lipped out. Tap in for bogey. Wie said later that the sequence left her "super pissed off" and "ready to bite someone's head off."

But while the greens baffled Wie, the course's length strangled just about everyone else. A final-hole birdie put her 1-under for the day, 6-under for the championship, and only one shot out of the lead going into the final round. Despite her putting woes, Michelle Wie's length and crisp iron play had kept her in the hunt.

Her analysis: "I feel like this course owes me a really good round."

Fans ringed the first hole on Sunday to see the parade of women's golf stars tee off. But Michelle Wie began with a thud. She completely misjudged her first approach shot, flew the green, and bogeyed to slip to 5 under. She lingered there after the next 10 holes, and found herself needing to make up two strokes in the final eight holes. It was now or never.

Eleven was a 596-yard behemoth, but Wie cut the distance down to size with a boomer. A good 300 yards away, a 55-year-old Southern Baptist minister from Savannah named Leonard Small stood along the ropes and stared incredulously when a ball rolled past where he stood. "If you can hit it that far as a 16-year-old," Small said, "it don't matter if you're a boy or a girl. You a bad man."

The bad man had something like 260 yards to the green. She pured a fairway wood that bounced twice in front of the green and rolled onto the front of the putting surface. The crowd was almost too stunned to applaud. A two-putt birdie from 35 feet put Wie within two strokes of leaders Se Ri Pak and Karrie Webb.

She blistered another perfect drive on 13, a par 4, and put her second shot pin high. But she still had a knee-knocking 35-footer up over a swale and back down to the hole. She stood over her ball, gave her line one last look, and swung her putter. The ball climbed the hill and started racing down the slope, closing distance and gaining speed as the gallery began to stir. When the ball vanished into the hole, the crowd exploded.

One stroke off the lead. Two rockets on 15, a par 5, left her a 70-foot chip. ("Oh, Lord, not another one," her supporters must have said to themselves, given what they'd seen of her chipping up until now.) This time, though, she chipped beautifully, stopping her ball within 3 feet of the cup. She made the birdie putt.

The next hole had baffled her since Thursday. Only 330 yards long, it seemed reachable, at least to Michelle Wie. Tempted as always, Wie hit a 5-wood on each of her first three visits, and missed the fairway all three times. This time, she took an iron and split the landing area. She had only 135 yards left, but she startled everyone in the vicinity by losing her wedge to the right of the green. She recovered with a soft lob that rolled to 4 feet. But putts from that range had victimized Wie all week. This one caught the right edge, did a full 360°, and trickled back toward her. The crowed gasped. Bogey.

Her face blank, Michelle Wie walked up the stairs to the tee box of 17, a 171-yard par 3. Steady despite what just happened, she landed an 8-iron within 15 feet and two-putted for her par. She then looked out at the large leaderboard for help.

She got it. Se Ri Pak bogeyed 18, dropping her into a tie with Karrie Webb at 8 under. Cristie Kerr (6 under) and Ai Miyazato (7 under) also finished strong. Wie had come away from the 388-yard par-4 final hole with birdies three times during the tournament. One more would put her in a play-off.

The fourth time wasn't a charm. She pulled her drive dangerously near a water hazard on the left. She stayed dry but had a tricky stance for her second shot. Expressionless, Michelle stepped up and nailed a low screamer that found its way on, but left her 60 feet away from birdie and a play-off. She gave it a ride, but the ball slid 4 feet past the cup.

Four feet. Her nemesis distance all week. As if on cue, she missed yet another for a final three-putt bogey.

Wie walked off the course without a trace of emotion on her face. A William Morris representative, Jill Smoller, greeted her and then patted the sweat off her brow with a tissue. (The fan who gave the tissue to the rep asked for it back, thinking it might make a nice souvenir.) Wie then faced the press. She knew the story before the first question got asked.

"It's very frustrating," she said. "I wasted a lot of shots."

Once again, Michelle Wie was Miss Almost. But this near miss was especially revealing. She ranked first in greens in regulation all week (80 percent), but once she got there, it was a different story. She finished 139th in putting.

She blew the tournament on the greens.

Later, Wie was adamant that she had "hit every putt right where I wanted to." But that was exactly the problem. Her eyes lied to her when she needed them most. And she wasn't allowed to consult a caddy, Greg Johnston, who'd helped Juli Inkster win that same tournament in 1999 and again in 2000.

Pride was getting in the way of winning.

15

Top Five

The fatigue and frustration of Canoe Brook and Bulle Rock cleared by the end of June, leaving a huge question: what would it be like if Wie listened to her caddy, focused on one event at a time, and putted with even a little bit more consistency?

The answer came at the 2006 U.S. Women's Open, at the Newport Country Club in Rhode Island.

Wie's opening press conference was almost as entertaining as her golf. She smiled broadly and eagerly tackled questions both serious and strange.

Q: What motivates you?
A: I just want to use my good golf to make a better world, to have positive influences on other people's lives.

Q: Would you rather make a PGA cut or win an LPGA tournament?
A: I'll DO both, and I'll tell you which is better.

Q: What about your putting problems?
A: I feel like every putt I make, every putt I miss, and every putt that goes around the toilet bowl, it's one step closer to being a better putter.

Q: Are you still growing?
A: I don't think I'm growing. I dearly hope to God that I'm not growing. I don't want to grow anymore.

Q: How do you feel about moving away from Hawaii before going to college?
A: That would be giving up my friends. That would be giving up my sixteen-year-old life, and I don't want to do that.

Q: What's it like to be so famous?
A: It's not like I'm a movie star. People don't recognize me when I go to a movie theater and stuff. Well, sometimes I am, sometimes I'm not. People in Hawaii are pretty much used to me by now. I don't get bothered a lot when I'm out. Occasionally I have a couple of fans come up and want to meet me and have my autograph, and that's pretty cool.

Q: What about not being a member of the LPGA Tour yet?
A: I feel like a freelancer. It almost reminds me of a newspaper, where you have your staff writers and then you also have your freelance writers. I'm like the freelance writer.

Q: Do you think your example will bring more girls into the game?
A: I think that girls are starting to realize that we can throw out our Barbies and start playing sports. People might think golf's a pansy sport. You're walking five miles every day if you're playing eighteen holes. I think that's a great way of being fit.

Q: Does your school have a dress code?

A: Well, it's not really a uniform, which is the worst part. If it was like a skirt and a tie and a vest thing, I would wear it, because it's a uniform. But we get to wear our own jeans. It's really weird. We have to wear like a shirt, it's like a regular T-shirt, they have a little Punahou mark on it, and they charge you a lot to buy it. I mean, obviously I'm not very happy with the dress code. Punahou, if you hear this, please take away the dress code.

Michelle Wie said she wanted to make the world a better place, and she wanted to win an LPGA Tour tournament *and* make a PGA Tour cut, though she didn't specify in what order. Maybe she didn't care. She wanted to do it all without giving up her 16-year-old's life, and without making any commitment to the LPGA Tour—that is, she would not petition for the right to compete in its Q-school.

Michelle Wie, it seemed, wanted everything without giving up anything.

Critics claimed she had not earned her way to Newport. Her final-round 82 at in the Open at Cherry Hills the year before had dropped her to a tie for 23rd, too low to qualify for an exemption to the 2006 Open. The USGA rescued her again by reasoning that she would have qualified if she had played on the LPGA Tour.

Meanwhile, two South Korean players who did qualify, Meena Lee and Joo Mi Kim, forgot to fill out their applications. Both dissolved in tears when notified of the mistake, yet both sat home all weekend without any help from the tour to which they actually belonged.

"Michelle Wie can only help us," said veteran Pat Hurst, who would perform magnificently in Newport, "but I wouldn't want to change a rule just for her."

But this was not the Michelle Wie of earlier in the month.

This was a more energetic golfer, a fresh golfer not sapped emotionally and physically by trying to do too much at once. And she would give Open watchers a nationally televised display of great golf that they would not see again from her for a long, long time.

Rain and fog forced cancellation of play on Thursday, and Friday morning revealed a swamp masquerading as a golf course.

Machines had been buzzing since before dawn, trying to suck up water from the fairways. Bunkers still looked like ponds. Every footstep brought a squish and a spring. Three holes were closed off to everyone but players, caddies, and officials. (That meant B.J. and Bo would miss one of Michelle's tournament holes for the first time.) Wie asked for relief on the very first green, failed to get it, and then watched as her putt left a wake like a tiny motorboat.

There would be no dazzling golf played in Newport this weekend; the winner would survive by treading water, almost literally. Michelle hated playing in wet conditions. This would be a soggy ordeal.

But she had a new weapon in her bag. At a promotional appearance six weeks earlier in the summer for the 84 Lumber Classic, a PGA Tour stop Team Wie had booked in September, Michelle met John Daly. After watching her putt, Daly suggested that she switch to a slightly more lofted putter to provide a tad more topspin and a better roll. She took his advice. The new putter gave her a mental boost.

Greg Johnston, her caddy since the previous October, gave her another. Johnston had been ordered by B.J. back at the LPGA to cease helping Michelle read greens. But at Newport, when she had trouble reading a break on the third hole, Wie asked Johnston for "some confidence." He stood behind her and offered his input. She made the putt to save par, a huge plus early in the round on a day when every par was a small victory. It was also a sign that Wie might be moving toward solving the one problem that had crippled her so much in the past. Not to mention putting a little distance between her and her father. She would go back to Johnston for "some confidence" from time to time the rest of the weekend.

ROUND 1 (FRIDAY): Michelle Wie shot a 1-under 70, leaving her just a stroke behind leaders Annika Sorenstam, Pat Hurst, Se Ri Pak, and amateur Jane Park. Pretty good company. And pretty good golf, considering the conditions. Best news of all: no three-putt greens.

ROUND 2 (SATURDAY): Wie's group started on the back side, and she was 1-under through the first six holes and still near the top of the leaderboard. Then, on a 185-yard par 3 with a narrow shard of a green protected on the left by a deep bunker, her tee shot found the sand—or, more precisely, the muck. Two shots to get out, two putts to get down. Double bogey. She made the turn at 1 over—not bad, all things considered.

Seven holes later Michelle Wie got one of those strokes back with the most incredible golf shot she hit all season.

The par-4, 359-yard 7th hole was nasty, both in its treat-ment of golfers and in its condition. A pond fronted the green, and the whole left side of the fairway looked like a rice paddy. Wie pulled her 3-wood to the left side, leaving her 155 yards from the green. As it came to rest in casual water—casual mud, really—she was entitled to a free drop. Johnston turned to usher some fans away, and when he turned back, he saw her ball in a different but equally messy spot. He looked up at Wie. "That's not your drop, is it?" Wie met his stare: "Uh, yeah!"

The task she faced was formidable: not only extricating the ball from the slop, but sending it over a water hazard to a pin cut right beyond it, with the mud precluding any thought of landing the ball and drawing it back. This shot would be like lobbing a grenade, one that could go two feet and explode in her face.

"Eight?" Wie asked.

"If it's right, it's right," Johnston said, neglecting to mention what would happen if it was not right. Johnston hated letting a player take such a preposterous risk—playing away from the water hazard and going for the green on the third shot was the safe move—but he knew by now that Wie wasn't into "safe." ·

Earlier in the week, during a practice round, the two had disputed about what club to use on a par 3. Wie went against Johnston and missed the green. Then she tried again and missed again. Johnston just looked at her. Wie hit a third shot and stuck it close. Then she turned to look at Johnston and said, "Told you it was the right club."

So Johnston stood back as Wie locked in on the ball. It was the perfect Wie moment: go for it all, don't consider failure as a possibility, and assume the best outcome. *This is either gonna be really good,* Johnston thought, *or really, really bad.*

• It was really good: pin high, 12 feet from a birdie.

B.J. Wie let out a roar that could be heard in some areas of Massachusetts. Michelle darted ahead to the green, rushing as always. Behind her she left a wide swath of ick on the fairway grass. After her tricky downhiller dropped, she walked quickly off the green, announcing in a near laugh, "That was *ri-di-cu-lous!*"

"She has no fear," David Leadbetter said after Saturday's round. "I know it's going to happen at some stage. It's when, not if. And when she takes that last step, it's Katie bar the door."

Michelle Wie entered the final day of the 2006 United States Women's Open at even par, two strokes behind and playing one group ahead of Annika Sorenstam.

Sunday's 36-hole ordeal would be the most taxing day of golf in her life. The 36-hole sectional qualifier for the U.S. Open had been grueling, but at Newport she'd be in the hunt for a major championship, with packed galleries, a national television audience—and only about 20 minutes for lunch. (At the sectional qualifier, she had more than an hour to unwind, rest, and eat.).

At least this time her group included Jane Park, a Korean American amateur from UCLA who was a genuine friend. They chatted as they walked up the fairways, while playing partner and defending British Open champion Jeong Jang looked lost in her own world. All three heard waves of cheering chasing them all over the course: for Annika Sorenstam and Pat Hurst behind them, and for Se Ri Pak and Juli Inkster up ahead. (That quartet would end with the best rounds of the morning: 71, 69, 69, 71.)

The course continued to take victim after victim, with top names bogging down in the mushy rough, then slipping into black numbers, and finally fading into oblivion. This wouldn't be exactly a showcase for many of the brightest young stars in the LPGA firmament. Some scores after three rounds: Paula Creamer (+6), Morgan Pressel (+12), and Natalie Gulbis (+8). Also withering in the morning's heat and mud: Lorena Ochoa (+10) and Ai Miyazato (+6).

Only the brainy and cool veterans of similar campaigns survived as noon drew near—Sorenstam, Hurst, and Inkster. And one other player who had virtually no experience at all with such extreme conditions: Wie.

ROUND 3 (SUNDAY MORNING): Michelle hit 10 of 14 fairways and all four of the par-3 greens to finish up exactly where she started, at even par. But considering the leaderboard was like the climactic scene in *Titanic,* with people vanishing almost by the minute, even par was impressive.

ROUND 4 (SUNDAY AFTERNOON): Wie barely had time to change outfits before returning to the fray, but the wear of the day didn't seem to be taking a toll. Sorenstam was another matter: she sent a message with birdies on the first two holes of the final 18.

Wie fell 3 back on 6, then needed a brilliant sand shot to save bogey on 9. On 12, she found herself looking at a 15-footer with maybe 2 feet of break, for an unlikely birdie. The ball wandered out toward the water and then swung back in, making it seem almost as if the hole had moved to grab it. Then it disappeared, and the grandstands shook.

Bonus: Sorenstam finished her front nine with double-bogey, bogey, bogey, and Wie was suddenly in a tie with her for first.

Michelle Wie had now been in a first-place tie on the back nine of all three majors of the season. But just as at the LPGA Championship, she followed an energizing birdie with a demoralizing bogey by finding the right bunker on the 13th, a 181-yard par 3, after coming up short with a too-tentative swing in the claylike sand, and two-putting once she finally made the green.

Meanwhile, Sorenstam birdied 10, 15, and 16, and 17 to finish even for the round and the tournament. Pat Hurst finished 2 under on the day to force a play-off. Michelle could only par out and tie for third with Pak and Stacy Prammanasudh at 2-over.

Michelle Wie grinned broadly making her final putt of the day, then walked side by side with Jane Park off the 18th green and toward the clubhouse. On her way up the path, Wie tiptoed over to Park and slapped her on the behind before darting away. Park followed, and the two scampered by the practice green like siblings in an airport terminal.

Michelle didn't seem the least bit bothered that, once again, she hadn't been able to close the deal. "I felt like I played awesome today," Wie told the media after the final round. "This time, I played awesome to the end."

She did. Except for a T-26th in the British Open, Wie finished in the Top 5 of every women's tournament she had entered in 2006, something no one on the LPGA Tour could say. She was one of only four players to earn more than $300,000 in the season's first three majors, the others being Hall of Famers Pak, Sorenstam, and Webb.

You could make the case—and her supporters did—that in 2006 Michelle Wie was the most consistent female golfer in the world. And she was *16 years old,* remember. All she had to do was keep the momentum going and she would be a cinch to win one of these majors and quiet the critics.

But other commitments got in the way.

Out of Focus

B.J. Wie never wasted time, never dawdled, never delayed. And yet the schedule for Michelle's first season as a professional took him a long time to complete. He had so many decisions to make, about so many tournaments, on three different continents. It took him deep into the winter of 2005–6 to finalize everything. And even then, he tinkered all the way into the summer.

Michelle ended up playing in more tournaments than originally scheduled. And one of the added tournaments was the HSBC Women's World Match Play Championship, held July 6–9 at Hamilton Farm Golf Club in Gladstone, New Jersey. The tournament had a hefty purse—$2 million—and a field that included all of the best LPGA players, but it made no sense whatsoever for Michelle, as it came only days before her trip to Illinois for the John Deere Classic, where she would try once again to make the cut in a PGA Tour event.

What was B.J. Wie thinking?

• • • • •

Things started well: Michelle won her first three matches against Candy Hannemann, Christina Kim, and Se Ri Pak. That set up a quarterfinal match with bomber Brittany Lincicome on a sweltering Saturday afternoon. But signs of exhaustion showed up before that match even got started.

"She's not much of a talker," Pak said after their match. "Me, I was having fun with my caddy. She wasn't really talking at all. We weren't having any conversation at all, but this is a match game. It was a little weird, but that's fine. She wanted to win."

Frostiness during match play happens all the time, but silence after rounds was unheard of from Wie. Ross Berlin approached her about a post-round media session, and Michelle said flatly, "I'm not doing any interviews."

No one could blame her. She barely had time to eat, change, and get ready for her afternoon match. For the third time in a month, she would play more than 30 tournament holes in one day. Wie was almost always accommodating. Perhaps she was just tired and needed a little time to relax. Or was there something deeper going on?

Michelle's opponent in the quarterfinal round was Brittany Lincicome, the only LPGA Tour player with Wie-like distance off the tee. A big-smiling, big-bopping, blue-eyed blonde from Florida, Lincicome—then in only her second year on the Tour—once described herself to a reporter as "nice and bubbly and willing to do anything for everybody." After taking the lead in the first round of the 2004 U.S. Women's Open when she was just 18, Lincicome spotted her mom in the crowd and began bawling right there on the fairway on her way to a 5-under 66.

"Just to see my dream coming true," she said at the time, "is an awesome feeling."

Several young golfers on the LPGA Tour have girl-next-door looks, but Lincicome has a girl-next-door personality as well. Her parents teach preschool, and her hobbies include fishing and Texas Hold'em. Her head covers at the HSBC were a fish, a turtle, and a pig, all with their mouths swallowing the woods.

Both players obliterated their first drives, and both had easy approach shots to the green. If this turned into a putting contest, and it had all the earmarks of doing so, it did not bode well for Wie. Sure enough, Lincicome dropped a beautiful left-to-right birdie putt on the first hole to go 1 up. She never looked back. Wie couldn't look ahead to the par 5s to right the ship the way she had against Pak. They made the turn with Lincicome 2 up, and then on 10 the Floridian made birdie to go 3 up. Wie was cooked, and she knew it.

She didn't take it well. After 3-putting 13 to go 4 down, she tried and failed to sweep her ball up with her putter. Caddy Greg Johnston grabbed the ball and tossed it to her, and Wie dropped it. But instead of leaning over to grab the ball, she walked away and left it for her caddy to pick up.

Lincicome noticed. She had played with Wie the year before, at the U.S. Open, and Michelle had chatted all day long, even going on a rant about how girls can wear short shorts at her school but the administration was threatening to put an end to that. This time, Wie was almost silent. "Maybe she was tired and didn't want to be there," Lincicome said. "She wasn't herself."

They halved 14, meaning Wie had to win the remaining four holes to tie the match. She didn't. On 15, Wie found another bunker and smashed her shot into the lip. She whipped the club in anger. It was over. Lincicome won, 4 and 3.

Once again, Wie's face glistened with fatigue. It had been a long couple of weeks, and now she would go straight to the Midwest for a PGA event. In the press tent she told writers she "had a lot of bad breaks" and that Lincicome "had a couple shots better than me." Outside, she scribbled a few autographs without expression.

Asked afterward if beating Wie made her win more special, Lincicome didn't hesitate: "Oh, it was huge. That was great."

But the press didn't stop there. Reporters seemed to enjoy the moment just as much, asking Lincicome not about her club selection or strategy but about why Wie didn't concede certain short putts. As it turned out, Lincicome wondered the same thing.

"I gave her a bunch of stuff," she said. "My match in the morning took forever, so I was trying to speed things up, giving 2- and 3-footers. A couple times I was looking at the putt and I'm like, why didn't she give me that?"

Reporters kept the fire lit, asking more about Wie's demeanor.

Lincicome was ready to accommodate: "I thought she would talk more but she honestly didn't. I would tell her 'good shot' and she would say nothing in return. Maybe she was just focused. Maybe I was messing her up by trying to talk to her, but yeah, she really wasn't talking a lot."

And what about the "bad breaks" Wie talked about?

"I don't remember there being any bad kicks. She had a couple putts where she blew it by."

The final salvo came not in response to a question about Wie but in response to a question about herself that was a thinly veiled question about Wie: would Lincicome ever consider playing against men?

"Like people have said out here," she replied in a measured tone, "if you can't beat Annika, you don't need to go play another tour."

Later, Lincicome elaborated: "You make the cut at a PGA event? Congratulations. But there's not so much she can do beyond that. She'll never be 50th on the money list. She'll never win."

Tiger Woods' ambition also drew ire at first. PGA Tour pros fumed when he bragged early on about being able to win a tournament with his "C game." But resentment ebbed when the PGA Tour renegotiated its television contract up from $90 million to $140 million shortly after Woods won his first Masters.

Wie had similar potential. Early-round coverage of the HSBC soared 68 percent over the year before, but weekend viewership on CBS—after Wie was eliminated—rose only 12 percent. And the crowds disappeared almost completely the day after Wie left. (The following year, with Wie not entered, the tournament seemed completely deserted.)

But because Wie did not join the LPGA, did not seem to want to join the LPGA, rarely paid homage to LPGA veterans who paved the way for her, and made little effort to cultivate personal relationships with young players on the Tour, her actions—or inaction—got construed as arrogance. She was winning prize money that would otherwise have been earned by full-time Tour members, and the LPGA Tour wasn't able to cash in on the "Wie Effect" the way the PGA Tour had with Woods.

Michelle Wie called herself a "freelancer," but to a growing element within the LPGA Tour she was merely a freeloader. Her aloofness tracked all the way back to practice rounds in Hawaii, when playing partners would actively search for Wie's lost balls but then discover that the girl and her parents weren't interested in returning the favor. It galled Tour members when Wie had told *60 Minutes* two years earlier that "if I just play in the women's tournaments, and I just play them over and over again, I think I'll get bored with golf." Plenty of Wie watchers felt that the girl and her family behaved as if she were entitled to special treatment.

People easily spotted the "I" in Wie. But "we"? Not so much.

At the John Deere Classic in July, Wie faced not only the pressure of trying to make a PGA Tour cut after four unsuccessful tries but also physical pressure. A hip strain required several trips to the medical trailer during the week, and there was the wrist. The pre-tournament press conference brought more than the usual number of tough questions. When a reporter from Hawaii asked why she hadn't spoken to Brittany Lincicome at the HSBC, Wie flatly said, "I don't talk in match play. It's a lot more intense. You have to win or not play the next day."

Then a South Korean man in the front row of the room launched into a broken-English rant that finally culminated by questioning Wie's "mental toughness." Wie lowered her brow just slightly. "I'm pretty mentally tough," she said. "That's not the reason I'm not winning tournaments."

Her first season had already included two tournaments in Hawaii (Sony and the Fields Open), two in California (Kraft Nabisco and Samsung), one in Japan (Casio), and three in the Eastern time zone (LPGA, the U.S. Open, and now HSBC). After the John Deere, Wie would have three tournaments in Europe (Evian, Women's British Open, Omega Masters) and one more PGA Tour event in the Eastern time zone (84 Lumber). Also, U.S. Open qualifying efforts in Honolulu and New Jersey. Plus multiple trips to New York City and Los Angeles for commercial appearances.

Oh, and completing her junior year in high school.

The Michelle Wie of the second half of the 2006 golf season was a completely different person from the engaging, eloquent 16-year-old who'd charmed the ink stains off the press in Newport. This one exhibited no energy, no enthusiasm. This one endured questions from the press, but there was no banter, no humor. Just get it over with.

Understandable, given her work overload. She'd been away from home for nearly two months and had nearly another month to go before returning to Hawaii. She hardly took a day away from the practice range. Plus there was a full load of schoolwork, a driver's test, and an application to Stanford. One William Morris agent, Jill Smoller, tried to get her to the mall on occasion just to give her a break, but there never seemed to be any time.

Life had become a heavy lift for Michelle Wie by the end of the summer. When asked whom she would call if she made the cut that week, she answered, "I don't call anyone; my friends don't care." She meant the comment as a sort of joke, but it underscored a poignant reality: during a long and trying summer of travel, she had no one to confide in other than her parents and a Florida-based sports psychologist.

The girl from Hawaii was on her own little island. And despite her much-improved play, the waves seemed to eat away at the beach a little more each week.

On Thursday morning, July 13, Michelle Wie—decked out in long pants, as demanded by the PGA Tour dress code—walked onto the TPC Deere Run in Silvis, Illinois, just outside of East Moline and only a few miles from the Mississippi River. The temperature was already in the mid-80s and on the way up, with punishing humidity. Welcome to the middle Mississippi Valley in high summer.

The gallery, dotted with older folks seated in lawn chairs, some wearing flower-print dresses, hushed as Wie appeared, only to erupt in applause as she walked to the tee box on the

10th hole. She wore khaki pants, and instead of funneling her ponytail through the back of her cap as she usually did, she had wrapped it in a bun. From a distance, she might have been a tall, lean young man.

Wie planted her white tee in between two toy John Deere tractors that served as tee markers and ripped a perfect drive. Off she went into the haze, with PGA Tour hangers-on Jeff Gove and Daisuke Maruyama.

Seventy-seven strokes later, her day ended at 6 over par, leaving her no chance in hell of playing on the weekend.

Perhaps that would turn out to be a blessing in disguise. She was obviously exhausted. And hurting. On her last two holes of the day, she bent at the waist and massaged her thighs between shots. She'd visited the medical trailer again before the round for help with her hip, but she was in pain. David Leadbetter had explained Wie's putting struggles as a function of not playing enough. But now she had a new problem: she was playing too much.

At around noon on Friday, just before Michelle Wie's tee time, five guys stood in a row by the concession area, each wearing a Nike golf hat and carrying a beer can in a coconut-shaped beverage holder. Each had on a sleeveless white T-shirt with black lettering. When they stood side by side in the right order, the letters spelled out UN BE WIE AB LE!

The buddies had planned the stunt for three weeks, said 31-year-old Steve Pennock, who admitted he was "a little hesitant this morning." A few sips of courage, plus the laughter and support from fans at the course, cleared that up fast.

"It's neat for her to try to get into this," Pennock said. "She's been putting up with a lot of flak."

Unfortunately, the sips of courage ended up dooming their

effort, as the "WIE" guy hustled to the portable toilets just before Wie noticed the group along the ropes. She tried to read the UN BE AB LE! message but then turned to keep walking. But at least the guys got noticed; Wie's gallery lined up tee to green.

The mercury inched up toward 90 degrees as the sun crept across the sky. Fans held umbrellas and waved programs like gospel churchgoers. Michelle herself forced down a large spaghetti lunch that wasn't sitting right, and caddy Greg Johnston could tell on the practice green that she didn't feel well. Johnston, who'd sooner gnaw off his own arm than admit to feeling pain on a golf course, did everything he could to encourage his player to beat back the discomfort.

But as the day wore on, it became clear that Wie lacked the energy she'd brought to earlier tournaments. Now she had a wrist problem and a hip problem, plus the notable absence of the joy she usually showed on the course, in addition to a bout of nausea, along with a whopping great stomachache. And she would have to push herself through the growing heat on a hilly 7,200-yard course. In the shade by the fifth green, she sat bent over on her bag and rubbed her stomach.

Wie got to the sixth tee and immediately drifted over to a cooler, where she stopped, grimaced, and once again rubbed her stomach. Fans began to realize something was wrong.

She took out her driver and split the fairway—nothing the matter there—but as soon as she got to her ball, she crouched over again. Johnston encouraged his player to endure, but the ache only deepened and the symptoms only spread. Wie made par, then walked quickly by a gaggle of little girls whose faces sank at seeing their idol in pain. At the seventh tee, Wie grabbed her stomach. The crowd murmured with speculation: indigestion . . . menstrual cramps . . . heat exhaustion . . . dehydration. A marshal offered her a bottle of water, but Wie waved it off. Ross Berlin, within shouting distance as always, leaned over the rope to ask the marshal what was the matter. As she got to the seventh green, a doctor appeared.

Wie played on, now walking slowly and gingerly, almost like a sleepwalker. After hitting her approach shot to the 8th green, she turned away from the shot and the gallery. The color leaked from her face.

Amazingly, her game hardly suffered. She made her birdie putt on 8 to bring her back to even par for the afternoon, and a wave of cheers went up. But Wie made no fist pump, and seemed to drag herself to the hole to retrieve her ball.

Hitting first on 9, she bisected the fairway, then sat down on her bag and put her hands to her face. "Oh no," said one reporter to another, "she's gonna be sick." Wie wobbled off to the tall grass near the tee box, her outstretched hand just beyond her nose. She trod into the weeds. A cameraperson hustled over, zooming in.

Wie held back the nausea, but convulsed as if ready to burst into tears. She made her way back to the fairway and to her ball, still in a near stumble. Michelle told Johnston she was going to stop after she finished the hole. Johnston realized he couldn't say anything to make his player feel any better, and walked by her side toward the green. After putting out for a par, Wie straggled off the green.

That was it: WD after nine holes of Round 2 of the 2006 John Deere Classic.

A TV reporter wandered over, and Wie shook her head, saying, "I really can't do any press right now." She sat in a waiting cart and rode to the medical trailer with Bo for what would be her third visit there in as many days.

Reporters gathered around B.J. as he followed. He smiled and politely offered tidbits of reassuring information: "She was hanging in there but the pain was too much. . . . She got sick at the range. . . . She had a big lunch, more than usual."

The medical trailer door opened 20 minutes later, and

Michelle Wie was wheeled out on a gurney. She looked barely conscious but smiled softly. An EMT was by her side, holding an IV aloft. She was gently lifted into the ambulance. Bo joined her, and the doors closed behind them.

B.J. strode toward a dark van, smiled toward the press, and announced, "She's fine! Getting better!" Once he got into the van, his smile disappeared. It must have seemed clear to B.J. that this was caused by back-to-back tournaments and all the pressure she'd been under.

Two Wie-related press statements were distributed.

The first, from Team Wie spokesperson Ross Berlin, explained that Illinois state law required that Michelle Wie be taken to the hospital: "She suffered a number of different symptoms, including stomach pains, nausea, dizziness and breathing problems which worsened as the round continued. Michelle was diagnosed with heat exhaustion and is now resting and in very good spirits."

The second, from the PGA TOUR press office, was a one-page handout with the subject head, "Michelle Wie Statement after WD at the John Deere Classic." But then it read:

The PGA TOUR congratulates Michelle Wie on her historic accomplishment in making the cut at the John Deere Classic, the first female in more than 60 years to do so on the TOUR. Her quality of play over the first two rounds is a testament to her high level of performance and individual achievement. The PGA TOUR wishes her well in her play this weekend.

Henry Hughes
Senior Vice President and Chief of Operations
PGA TOUR

The press office had mistakenly pasted in the wrong release.

As Wie rested in the hospital, Gove and Maruyama finished their round. Reporters circled Gove, who had missed the cut by a single stroke. They began by asking him if the earlier scene was scary in any way.

"Scary?" Gove asked. "Why?"

Gove hadn't noticed Wie's illness. "She just said, 'I'm going to withdraw,' " he said. "That was good because she was holding us up again."

He went on:

> She's got a beautiful swing, but she's got her name on her bags, and she needs to be professional. And she's not there yet. She's got a little time. I know she's 16. But if she wants to play pro golf, she needs to learn how to act. She's got to learn to play faster and be a little more respectful of the other players, things of that nature. Just being ready to play. Realizing we were behind yesterday and not doing anything about it. Some of that's your [the media's] fault, giving her too much attention, too early.

The schedule wouldn't ease up.
The pain wouldn't let up.
And now the critics were lining up.

Circling of the Wolves

There is no obvious similarity between Michelle Wie and Old Muffin Face.

One is a beautiful teenage Korean American. The other is a long-dead South African who won his country's Open championship, served in its military during World War II, and appeared on the American golf scene in the late 1940s in his necktie, plus-fours, and Ben Hogan hat. Wie strides down the fairways like a runway queen, smiling and waving and full of vim; Old Muffin Face shuffled his way from tee to green. He shook hands nervously and said almost nothing. His perpetual droop earned him the nickname. His real name was Bobby Locke.

The differences extended to the game itself. Wie blasts perfect drives with a swing that TV analyst and former golf great Johnny Miller called one of the five best in the world. Locke's swing could not have been uglier. He hooked every drive so badly that he aimed as if he wanted to lose his ball out of bounds to the right.

But Bobby Locke could putt. Man, could he ever putt. Fellow countryman Gary Player once said, "One 6-foot putt, for my life? I'll take Bobby Locke. I've seen them all, and there was never a putter like him. In the 100 or so competitive rounds I played with him, I saw him three-putt just once." As Locke always said—and yes, he's the one who said it first—"You drive for show but putt for dough."

Sam Snead once told a story about how Locke began tipping his hat when a long putt still had 25 feet left to roll before falling into the cup. Slammin' Sam played Locke in a series of 16 exhibition matches and won only twice. Putt for dough, because Snead never put a tee into the ground without a little action on the side.

One thing brings Michelle Wie and Old Muffin Face into the same sentence: both exhibited an air of supreme confidence that got under the skin of a lot of people.

Locke showed up for his first Masters in 1947 and teed off without a single practice round. He finished 14th. Then he won four tournaments in five weeks, finished the year with seven victories, and rose all the way to third on the money list. The next year, he won twice, including one victory by a PGA Tour–record 16 strokes.

But it was his unwillingness to tip his hat to American golfers—long putts that he knew were going to drop, sure; fellow pro golfers this side of the Atlantic, not so much—that made his American peers angry. Locke respected Ben Hogan, but said little about anyone else in the United States. Then, in 1949, Locke won the British Open and decided to stay and play in Europe rather than come back to the United States to fulfill tournament commitments. The PGA banned him.

No one could deny Locke's talent, but everyone had a say

about Locke's way. He won three more British Opens but never won fame or a big following in the States. In 1988, *Golf Magazine* named Locke the greatest putter in golf history, but that was a year after he died. Locke was simply too different, and too misunderstood, to win the permanent respect of mainstream golfers.

"There's a lot of resentment of change in golf," says golf writer John Hopkins of *The Times* of London. "Bobby Locke got huge resentment because he took players' money. That's now applying to Michelle. It's narrow-minded and unfair. Look, she's . . . potentially the best the women's game has ever seen. And she might evolve into one of the world's best golfers. She is the most prodigious talent that I or anyone else has ever seen."

And yet Europe didn't catch Wie fever as much as the rest of the world did. England, especially, is still a place where girls feel uncomfortable taking up a sport so steeped in tradition and rules. Far more than in America, golf in England is considered an elitist game.

"Kids here find golf very intimidating," says Hopkins. "There are so many rules about when you can play and when you can't play. There are rules about what clothes you can and can't wear. And golf has not done a good job getting minorities. It's still mainly white."

So when 16-year-old Michelle Wie crossed the Atlantic to play in the 2006 British Women's Open, she was going up against the best women golfers in the world *and* a century of tradition. Besides her magnificent swing, she carried with her an approach to golf that Europeans, and especially Brits, deemed inappropriate, especially in one so young.

She was, in her own special way, a modern-day Bobby Locke.

Except for the putting part.

• • • • •

The 2006 British Women's Open began on August 3 at Royal Lytham & St. Annes, a venerable links course in Lancashire, on England's far west coast. But Wie and most of the LPGA Tour contingent planning to tee it up there first stopped in France for the Evian Masters, contested at Evian-les-Bains, the consensus pick as the most beautiful tournament host town on the women's circuit on either side of the Atlantic.

The big-payday event ($2.6 million in 2006) takes place on a 6,171-yard course carved out of a mountainside sloping down to Lake Geneva, not far from the Swiss border. The Wies dined outside as much as they could, as temperatures soared into the 90s every day of the tournament. The weather at the Evian Masters, played from Wednesday to Saturday, would make the John Deere Classic seem mild.

Wie came prepared. She announced only seconds into her pre-round press conference that "I've learned my lesson" and would spend most of the blazing-hot week walking up fairways with a giant Nike umbrella in one hand and a water bottle in the other. And once the tournament began, she also seemed to make an effort to talk with playing partners, something she'd virtually stopped doing.

On Friday, for instance, Wie played with Canadian Lorie Kane and told her a story about how a phone rang during one of her rounds. "This phone rings, right?" Wie said, her umbrella throwing some shade over Kane as they walked. "I'm not happy. The marshal's like, 'Quiet please!' You know where the phone was?"

Kane, not breaking stride: "In his pocket?"

"Yeah!"

But aside from course courtesy, Wie didn't need to prove anything to anyone. She came into the Evian with eight Top-5 finishes in her previous 10 LPGA events, including four in five majors. The only two non-Top-5 finishes in that run were in the 2005 U.S. Women's Open, where she led the entire field before her final-round 82, and in the 2005 Samsung World Championship, where she would have finished fourth had not an infraction led to a DQ. Forgotten in the sniping of the HSBC and the heat exhaustion of the John Deere in July was the fact that no woman golfer save perhaps Lorena Ochoa was playing better in the summer of 2006 than Michelle Wie at age 16.

It seemed obvious to all, fans and critics alike: Michelle Wie was on the brink of her first victory as a professional.

The 17th hole looked like it belonged on a miniature golf course.

The green on the 100-yard par 3 sat far below the tee box, making it look like a ball could actually be thrown to within birdie range. (That's no typo, by the way: at 100 yards, the 17th at Evian-les-Bains is the shortest hole in professional golf.) Hitting the green required wedges and half swings and the touch of Phil Mickelson. Telephone wires hung over the tee box, giving the false impression that taking too high an approach would cause a shot to deflect off a wire.

The 18th, a par 5 reachable in 2, was where Wie did her best scoring for the week. But the 17th, visually simple but actually mind-bending, was where Wie's destiny lay.

She came to 17 for the first time on Wednesday at 2-under. She had two club choices: a 52-degree wedge or a 56-degree wedge. She took the 52, swung, and saw the ball scream toward the pin. "Down!" she yelled. "Down!" But the ball didn't listen; it bounced into the back bunker, a full 20 yards past the flag. She chunked her sand shot and made bogey.

Wie finished the first day at 3-under, tied with Annika

Sorenstam and three shots behind Lorena Ochoa, Mi Hyun Kim, and Australian Shani Waugh. But Thursday was even better: Wie made the turn at 6-under for the day and 9-under for the tournament, where she stood when she came to 17 with a shot to take the lead outright.

The day before, the 52-degree wedge went long into the sand. This time, the same club came up 40 feet short, but at least on the short grass. Two putts for par.

(Two putts that took forever to execute. Struck by the time Michelle Wie spent on the greens, a reporter on the scene had been timing her pre-putt routine: walk to the hole and back, examine the line from the side, crouch behind the ball, stand over the ball, remove the ball marker, address the ball, and putt. Elapsed time: two minutes plus.)

On Friday, Wie arrived at 17 at 3-under and 12-under for the tournament, an all-but-sure bet to play in the final group on Saturday. This time, she grabbed the 56-degree wedge . . . and fired over the green. Poor chip. Two putts. Bogey.

Wie made birdie on 18, blasting her drive 335 yards and knocking a pitching wedge from 141 yards to inside 20 feet. She walked off the course one stroke behind the leader, Karrie Webb. Yes, she told the press afterward, she was pleased with her round. Yes, she was excited to be playing in the final group with Webb on Sunday. But her dander was still up about the 17th hole: she vowed to the press that she would not leave France without making a birdie there.

On the final day, Wie forged a two-shot lead over Webb through 11. Seven holes stood between Michelle and her first victory since the 2003 Women's Publinx. She was at the top of her game. She was closer than ever. Would this be the day?

Not so fast, said Webb, who fought back with a birdie on 12, a par on 13 as Wie went bunker to bunker for bogey, and a

15-foot birdie putt on 14. Suddenly Michelle Wie was a stroke down.

Along came 17.

Webb's tee shot landed about 18 feet short of the hole. Wie dropped her 56-degree wedge dead center, only 15 feet away from the birdie that the day before she'd vowed she'd make or take up French residency.

Webb, a winner of five majors on the LPGA Tour and one of its better putters, had an uphill try with a left-to-right break. She stroked the ball and watched it sidle slowly toward the hole. She began to lean forward, helping it. The ball dropped. So did Webb, to her knees. She pumped a fist and grinned.

Now Michelle was two back. She had to make this putt. She inspected it from every possible angle. She stepped away from the ball three times. She took nearly three minutes. Finally, she swung through. After so many oh-so-slight misreads on late putts over the course of the season, would Wie finally aim true?

No. The ball headed right at the hole. It had the right speed. It closed in. Then it leaked right and slid past six inches. A good putt, but not a Bobby Locke putt.

A birdie on the final hole brought Michelle Wie to within a stroke of a play-off for her first professional win. She had overcome her tendency to slip on the final day, but she still hadn't mastered the art of closing the deal.

On Karrie Webb's way back to the clubhouse, an acquaintance put an arm around her and said simply, "Thanks." Webb grinned, knowing what the gratitude was for: beating the kid. "I think I'll be hearing a lot of that," she confided later. Michelle Wie would still win a "Least Likely to Be Voted Most Popular Girl" contest in the LPGA.

Wie came up short again, but her shot making, self-discipline, nerves, and even putting had all improved over the course of the season. The soon-to-be high school senior had better marks on the year than Paula Creamer, Natalie Gulbis, Morgan Pressel, and the other youngsters on the LPGA Tour.

"Whatever she's doing," said Gulbis, "it's working."

The front nine at Royal Lytham & St. Annes begins in the town of St. Annes-on-Sea and wanders along a stretch of train tracks to the ninth green, which rests in the neighboring town of Lytham. Then the course halts, turns, and returns, usually into the wind, to the town where it began.

A classic links course, Royal Lytham has hosted 10 Open Championships (known as the British Open in America) and three Women's Open Championships since its founding.

A slashing wind off the Irish Sea is the course's principal feature, with cold, driving rain a close second. Michelle Wie dressed for her practice round in a ski hat, a thick jacket, and rain pants. The wind and rain were so nasty that she had to hit a 5-iron from 150 yards, normally an 8-iron at most for her. Wie gave up after 17 holes and went inside to eat lunch. She wobbled off the course with her cheeks so burned that she looked like a Christmas caroler from a Frosty the Snowman movie. "The wind beats you up," she said. "It feels like somebody's slapping you around."

Wie was well aware how close she was to winning. The near miss in France was almost reassuring. "It's very frustrating right after you finish playing," she said, "but if you look at the overall year, it's the best I've ever played."

Two weeks earlier, Tiger Woods had won his third British Open, at Royal Liverpool, by leaving his driver in the bag and depending on precision iron play. But Wie, whose game got weaker as the pin got closer, did not yet have the ability to morph from a power player into a precision performer.

Michelle Wie began her second British Open—the year before at Royal Birkdale she'd tied for third—on a decidedly ugly note: bogey, bogey, bogey.

She got a stroke back with a birdie at 8 to make the turn at 2-over, but on the 487-yard 11th aggressiveness and inexperience bit her in a situation where she was normally dominant: the tee box of a par 5. This fairly short one snaked around a large hill and through a minefield of bunkers. Iron-iron-pitch and she'd be putting for a birdie. But Wie, who never met a par 5 that didn't present an eagle opportunity, hit driver and yanked it into rough at the foot of the hill. After a quick once-over, Johnston counseled his boss to pitch out short, which would leave her an easy 100 yards to the green. *Say what? Not try to reach in two on a short par 5, just because you're in the rough? That's crazy talk,* her look told him.

So Wie slashed through the gunch, caught a flier, and watched her ball sail over the fairway and into the rough on the other side. *Deeper* rough. Another hard swing took her to a deep greenside bunker. She put her sand shot 12 feet past and missed the comebacker. Bogey. Make that bogey on a par 5.

Four bogeys and a solitary birdie left Wie 3-over and 6 strokes back of the leaders going into 18, which she birdied after a gorgeous 5-iron to 3 feet. Later, she expressed justified happiness with the way she'd fought and finished, but had she been able to adjust her mind-set earlier to fit the course, she might have ended the day far happier.

Object lesson: short-hitting Tour veteran Juli Inkster, who has a daughter Wie's age, danced around the course's myriad bunkers with her dazzling short game to finish the first round at a stunning 6-under.

Wie found 5 of Royal Lytham's 198 bunkers in the same round.

On Friday afternoon Wie came out fresher and much more precise. She didn't miss a green on the front, holding steady at even par on the day. And on her second shot at 11, where she'd bogeyed the day before, Wie hit a nice, low draw to the front fringe and made birdie to go under par for the day. She parred the next two holes and came to the par-4 14th with a chance to claw back into contention, as she had at the LPGA Championship.

Wie hit driver up the left side of the fairway, then pulled her approach shot into a bunker. She shook her head as she walked to the ball. Then she stepped down into the trap and Johnston noticed her ball resting just in front of a clump of something. "Is that a rock?" he asked her, hoping it was a loose impediment. The rules are slightly different in Europe: a golfer can remove a rock from a trap before swinging. In the States, that's forbidden. Wie replied: "No, it's moss."

Wie took her stance, careful not to disrupt the moss. Then, during her backswing, her wedge brushed against the clump and moved it slightly. She swung through, catching the moss, the sand, and the ball, which landed about 20 feet past the hole. She climbed out of the trap, two-putted for bogey, and moved on to the next hole.

Hundreds of miles away, at BBC headquarters, phones started ringing off the hook. Replays clearly showed Wie's infraction: moving a loose impediment on her backswing. She parred out to finish even on the day and still 2-over for the tournament, but as she walked off the 18th green toward the scorer's trailer, she was about to fall from the fringe of contending to the fringe of getting DQ'ed for signing an incorrect scorecard.

Jill Smoller, who had become a friend and confidant to Wie, put an arm around her shoulder and began speaking in a low and urgent voice. Wie's eyes widened. Then she nodded. She walked into the scorer's trailer.

Inside, a rules official explained to Wie that replays had caught her brushing the moss with her backswing. That would mean a two-stroke penalty. Wie pointed at the woman and said, "This is fucking bullshit."

A few minutes later, Wie exited the trailer. Her parents summoned her to the side, away from the media, and began questioning Michelle. "I didn't know," she told them. "I didn't know." There really wasn't anything more to say. She thought she could make contact with a loose impediment even on her backswing. She was wrong.

The two-stroke penalty tacked on to an otherwise decent round left her at 4 over par for the tournament, 10 strokes behind leader Juli Inkster.

A gaggle of reporters gathered around the scorer's trailer heard Wie explain that she thought that if she swung through an impediment on the downswing that striking it on the backswing was allowed. She vowed to hold her club "three feet" above the sand next time. "It's something you learn when you're 16," she offered, grinning. Asked if she had read *The Rules of Golf,* Wie responded with a dismissive laugh and said, "Well, they're not actually great reading material."

A couple of reporters chuckled. Others weren't amused. Michelle Wie, they thought, was playing a youthful-innocence card that had expired. She was too smart, too experienced, and too media-savvy to demean *The Rules of Golf* as not worth her time.

Certainly not on the record.

• • • • •

Saturday morning found Wie on the driving range, pounding iron shots into the distance, as B.J. stood close by, watching every swing and follow-through and shot arc. Johnston was not with them. The media tent crackled with reports of Wie receiving a "dressing-down" from her parents after her misinterpretation of the rules. How would she respond?

With an even par 72 to put her 11 strokes behind tournament leader (and eventual winner) Sherri Steinhauer, who shot 66. For the first time all year, she would go into Sunday in a women's tournament without a chance of winning.

Wie shot a final round 74—her third 74 of the week—to tie for 26th. For the first time since she started playing in professional tournaments, Michelle Wie wasn't invited to the media tent the entire week, although reporters did encircle her outside the scorer's trailer to ask once again about the bunker error.

"You're put under a microscope and every mistake is seen by thousands of people," she said. "Unfortunately, it's happened twice."

That morning, the *Daily Mail* had run a double-truck spread and full story on Wie. She was shown in two photos and described as "enchantingly elegant in black trousers, black shirt with a red belt and Chanel Eiffel Tower drop-earrings." And although the *Observer* did have a photo of leader and eventual winner Sherri Steinhauer, writer Dai Davies spent only three short paragraphs on the front-runner before veering into a full-on slam of the teen.

"Michelle Wie," wrote Davies, who has covered golf since the 1960s, "dressed in all black as if mourning a week of missed opportunities." He then used the words *contentious, ignorance,* and *astounding* in reference to Wie's reaction after she was penalized for the infraction. He wrote that Wie "threw a teenager's tantrum" in response to the ruling, and that she "had no right not to know" the rule.

"She is still at school," Davies continued, "still of an age where unappealing subjects have to be studied and the incentive in this instance is both financial—penalty shots cost money—and the maintenance of a good reputation."

Davies then took a sideswipe at B.J. Wie's money lust before finishing with this salvo: "Since his daughter turned professional on 11 October 2005, one informed estimate of her total income is $18 million. Sony and Nike have both contributed $5 million each; sufficient, surely, for a few dreary hours in front of the rulebook."

Michelle had a different view. "I think, strangely enough," Wie said to reporters after her final round, "that I learned more here this week than I did all summer."

What did she learn?

"How to play the game, really. Playing a links golf course really forces you to play golf. I learned to try and be patient out there."

But patience was never Michelle Wie's strong suit.

Greg Johnston had carried Wie's bag full-time for nearly a year, beginning with the Samsung World Championship. He had traveled to three different continents from his Virginia Beach home, and had dealt with bouts of silence from Michelle and bouts of anger from B.J. Wie. He had taken heat from a few golf writers who blamed him for Wie's struggles. And by the Evian Masters, Michelle and Greg had become more of a team than ever. He helped more with club choice and even with the occasional read on the greens. They talked and joked some on the fairways. Johnston thought their first season together had been a great success.

His opinion didn't count. The day after the Open, Johnston was eating a muffin at his gate in the Manchester airport prior to his flight home when Ross Berlin walked up and sat down. The agent appeared more somber than usual. "I got a call from B.J.," Berlin said. "I'm sorry to tell you, but you've been dismissed."

Johnston's eyes went wide: "*What?* You're kidding!"

Berlin wasn't kidding. The two just sat there. Berlin didn't know what to say. Neither did Johnston. Finally, Berlin tried to offer some sort of explanation. "They're moving in another direction," he said, but he clearly was clueless about exactly why the Wies had fired him. Johnston even tried to console Berlin, saying, "I'm sorry you had to be the one to tell me." That didn't make Berlin feel any better.

"My heart sank," Johnston said later. "I felt awful."

Eventually, the two men boarded the plane. They were on the same flight back to the States. Johnston sat and pondered what had just happened. "I didn't know what to think," he said. "Why and what happened and what didn't happen."

The decision, Johnston figured, had to have been spur-of-the-moment. B.J. had given him the course diagrams for the 84 Lumber Classic, on their September schedule, on the Tuesday before the British Open. Why would he do that if the caddy's days were numbered?

Caddies get fired all the time. Morgan Pressel had switched caddies only a few weeks before, and Lorena Ochoa would fire her bag man that same week in the middle of her best season ever. But usually the firing is done in person, instead of through a messenger. Especially one who couldn't explain why.

Neither Michelle nor B.J. nor Bo called to explain or say goodbye.

Weeks passed. Johnston didn't hear from the Wies. He debated calling them, if only to figure out why he got pushed out. The press release, handled not by William Morris but by Ken Sunshine Consultants, shed little light:

> Greg Johnston's hard work and dedication made him a great partner for Michelle, as he would be for any other golfer. His departure comes as part of Michelle's maturation as a golfer, part of which is learning from many different bright golf minds. We wish Greg the best, and are sure he will have a long and successful career.

Blather. Wie wasn't "learning from many different bright golf minds." The only two minds she learned from belonged to David Leadbetter and B.J. Wie. Wie's "maturation as a golfer" wasn't being hindered by Greg Johnston, one of the best caddies in the business. He had warned Wie before her two major mistakes of the season: the illegal drop at Samsung and the loose impediment violation at Royal Lytham.

Indeed, the last bit of golf advice Johnston gave Wie came on his last loop as her caddy. On the 15th hole, a par 5, Wie went for the green in two despite Johnston's urging to lay up and avoid the minefield of bunkers. Wie landed in two, needed two shots to get out of each, and three-putted for a triple bogey. A par on that hole would have tied her for 16th. Subtract the two-shot penalty for her encounter with the moss in the third round and she would have been all alone in 10th.

The reason B.J. Wie fired Johnston was because he wanted a caddy with PGA Tour experience. Michelle had handled the LPGA courses beautifully all season; at the more demanding venues for men's events, with their faster greens, she had struggled. Perhaps Johnston's relative unfamiliarity with layouts on the men's tour might have limited his ability to assist her, at least at first. At least that was B.J.'s rationale.

But the actual pluses and minuses of the decision mattered far less than the public fallout. For the first time, Team Wie had made an undeniably bad public relations decision: not necessarily the firing itself, but the handling of the firing. Up until the Johnston decision, criticism of the Wies' aloofness and arrogance seemed at least partially rooted in pettiness and jealousy. But having Berlin do their dirty work, and never once personally acknowledging Johnston's contributions, seemed to validate the charges. The move also indicated that Team Wie's impatience level was rising, not subsiding, Michelle's mantra about having "learned a lot" from yet another failure to win was getting stale.

The firing also demonstrated Michelle's growing tendency to blame external factors for her struggles on the course. As the season had gone on, she increasingly blamed "bad breaks" such as spike marks on greens, difficult lies in bunkers, or cell phones going off while she was lining up a putt. Every professional faces those obstacles on every golf course, but not everyone dwells on them as much as she did.

Greg Johnston had nothing to do with Wie's failure to win a tournament in 2006. In fact, he was an important reason why she came as close as she did so many times. "They got rid of the caddy," said Gary Gilchrist of B.J. and Michelle, "but they're going to have to take some responsibility sooner rather than later."

Writing in *Sports Illustrated,* E.M. Swift called the Wies' behavior a "pattern." He quoted Juli Inkster, who did not receive a call or e-mail or anything when the Wies hired Johnston away from her in the first place.

It would have been nice to get a phone call . . . saying this is what we're thinking of doing. I'd had Greg for 11 years. It's not like I was some rookie. But that's not the way they do things. Instead they gave him a take-it-or-leave-it in the middle of my season, right before the Solheim Cup. I don't blame him. He's got kids to think about. But that didn't sit well.

Swift then took over: "Excuses from the Wie camp have been piling up high. Bad luck. Bad bounces. A bee sting. Heat exhaustion. Too much golf. Too little golf. It's always something."

SI.com ran a poll alongside Swift's column, asking readers, "Are Michelle Wie's parents making a mistake with the way they're handling her career?" The Web site asked readers to check one of two possible answers:

No: She's still just a teenager.
Yes: She's turning into a spoiled child.

Of the more than 17,000 respondents, more than 15,000 (89%) said Yes.

The major public relations problem with Michelle Wie as she became more prominent centered on her alleged sense of entitlement.

- What gives her the right to skip junior golf?
- What gives her the right to play against men before she's proved herself against women?
- What gives her the right to earn millions without winning a tournament?
- What gives her the right to accept tournament exemptions and other LPGA benefits without making a concerted effort to promote the Tour or pay homage to its generations of stars?

- What gives her the right to talk about her dreams of qualifying for the Masters when she hasn't even made a PGA cut?

- What gives her the right to make light of *The Rules of Golf* after committing two major rules infractions in less than a year?

- And what gives her (or her parents) the right to fire a caddy she's had for almost a year without even the courtesy of a phone call?

The Wies themselves did little then and have done little since to answer these questions or even acknowledge them.

The truth is, Michelle Wie might never have become one of the greatest teen talents in sports history if she'd paid attention to all the admonitions to slow down. The customary "Caution: Go Slow" and "Yield Right of Way" signs in her sport annoyed her to no end.

So she ran through them.

"The *Titanic* Just Hit the Iceberg"

Jon Khil met Michelle Wie in 1999, when he was eleven and she was ten. A junior golfer who lived with his family in Manoa, a residential neighborhood a few miles east of Honolulu, Jon dropped by the nearby Olomana Golf Links one day to sit in on a golf clinic.

Michelle was teaching the class.

They became classmates, then good friends at Punahou. They shared an English class as freshmen and another as seniors. They read *Siddhartha* and *A Lesson Before Dying* together. They both loved Punahou. Their other bond, of course, was golf.

So as senior year went on and they saw more of each other, Khil got a chance to see the real Michelle Wie: "She has a great sense of humor. Always cracking jokes. A lot of fun to be around. She contributes to discussion a lot, and she likes to give her opinions. We've come to think of her as one of the leaders of the discussion."

Their friendship contained a lot of back-and-forth

kidding—he teased her about her unwillingness to play AJGA events—but when Wie began to struggle late in 2006 and the criticism mounted, Khil noticed that his friend didn't sulk.

"People have her wrong," he said. "They think she's some stuck-up person. She was under a lot of pressure and criticism. She told me she wants to follow what she feels is right, and she doesn't have a lot of self-pity."

Wie missed a lot of school to play in golf tournaments, but the two kept in touch by e-mail and Khil says he never picked up a hint of doubt from her: "I'm proud of the way she's able to handle the ups and downs. I turn on the TV and I see people bashing her and I think, 'I hope Michelle's not watching this.' The thing about the media is that it's very one-sided."

Khil was so inspired by his friend that he decided to write his college admission essay for Claremont McKenna on her. The essay was entitled "Leadership: Michelle Wie Shows That Possibilities Can Become Reality" and began by saying "There are many traits that make a successful leader. And Michelle portrays them." It then went on to talk about her many strengths, both physical and mental.

(Postscript: Khil ended up going to Macalester College in St. Paul, Minnesota.)

By unanimous agreement among others who knew her well in high school, Michelle Wie was compassionate, funny, opinionated, and full of energy. That was also the Michelle Wie her family and friends knew, and the Michelle Wie that reporters remembered from her days as an amateur.

But toward the end of her first pro season, that Michelle Wie flickered and faded from public view.

She was crying.

Michelle Wie came off the final green at the 2006 Omega

Masters in Crans-sur-Sierre, Switzerland, at 15 strokes over par. For two rounds. In both—78 on Thursday, 79 on Friday—her drives sprayed all over the place, her iron play was almost as erratic, and her short game brought no ballast. For the first time since 2003, she finished last in a tournament. But that had been at an LPGA Tour tournament in South Korea, the CJ Nine Bridges, when she was 13. The Omega Masters is a stop on the PGA European Tour—a men's event—and she was now 16.

She missed the cut by 14 strokes.

The world hadn't seen Wie on a golf course since the firing of Greg Johnston. Her new caddy, Andy Lano, had formerly worked for Kenny Perry and applied to haul Wie's bag without ever seeing her play. But his PGA Tour experience obviously didn't do Michelle much good, at least during their first time out together.

Yet thoughts that Wie's struggles at the Women's British Open would temper her big dreams were obliterated when she announced after playing a practice round with Sergio Garcia before the Omega Masters that she wanted to someday play for the U.S. Ryder Cup team: "I think it's totally possible."

Near-universal reaction from the golf world: "Yeah, sure."

A growing chorus of critics called for Wie to play on the LPGA Tour, period. Wie even took heat for her fashion. She played Friday in a mid-thigh-length black skirt with a short-sleeved black top. A German radio station reported that Omega, the tournament sponsor and a backer of Wie, had asked her to wear the short skirt. A Nike spokesman then chimed in, saying Wie's skirt length would be changed.

"I am pleased for the European Tour that we have gone ahead with this experiment, or should I say initiative," said George O'Grady, executive director of the European Tour, talking about the invitation to Wie to play in the Omega Masters. "But it will take some quiet persuading for this to happen again."

"I think it is time for this to stop," B.J. said after the second round. "But she is a very determined young woman and enjoys competing in the men's tournaments. As a parent . . . I don't regret her coming here to Switzerland to play, but I am disappointed with her results."

He wasn't quite done: "But if I was to tell her that enough is enough, she would not listen to me. She is a very stubborn girl, but as her father I do feel very sorry for her."

The fact is that Michelle was limited to playing eight LPGA Tour events on sponsor's exemptions until she was 18, at which time she could go through qualifying school and try to earn full membership. She could petition the Tour for earlier membership, as had Morgan Pressel, but Michelle or B.J. (or both) chose not to go that route. Now Q-school looked more and more like the only reasonable option.

"The *Titanic,*" said Gary Gilchrist after the fiasco at the Omega, "just hit the iceberg."

This didn't have to happen. Wie was clearly exhausted after the John Deere Classic, and she didn't seem any livelier at the Women's British Open. But instead of going home for a little decompression and rest after the British, she went to London, then New York, and then Los Angeles for commercial appearances. Even when she returned to Hawaii and began her senior year of school, she showed up on the first day of classes with a slip requesting time away from school to travel halfway around the world to Europe for the Omega Masters and then halfway back, to Pennsylvania for the 84 Lumber Classic. Both in September.

"My school like totally piled on the homework last week," Wie said at the Omega Masters pre-tournament press conference. "I had to bring much of it with me here to Switzerland. I wasn't able to practice like I usually do because I was working on this geography report."

Her wrist had not had time to heal. Her hip was hurting. Her tempo, always a sure thing whenever she stepped to a tee, seemed rushed, perhaps because of her father's determination that she must add distance to compete against men.

"She used to have a natural flow, a rhythm," said her first coach, Casey Nakama. "That's what she's gotten away from. She's jerky. She's trying to hit the ball too far."

"I think she's a little burned out," said family friend Lily Yao. "My advice to her is to take time off, go to school, focus, and rest. I think it's temporary, and I think it's the schedule. Not just the golf, but all the commercial work. That takes a toll on any human body."

Wie's psychologist, Jim Loehr, shared the same worry: "You can't play a major and then go right away and play a men's event. Can she go to Europe and race back? As young as she is, even the best athlete in the world can't easily do that."

But once again the Wies chose not to listen to the growing refrain. Perhaps that was because Michelle's critics, in B.J.'s words, "didn't understand the commercial imperatives."

But she didn't really have to play in either the Omega Masters or the 84 Lumber Classic. Omega, though a sponsor, did not insist on Wie coming in 2006. And 84 Lumber was run by a Wie family friend, Maggie Hardy Magerko, who dearly loved the family and Michelle. Surely she would have understood if Wie withdrew.

These two tournaments, like the HSBC match play event, brought huge risk and minimal likely reward. And yet, despite wrist pain and fatigue and Michelle's last year of high school ticking away, the family plunged ahead anyway. Wie shot a 14-over on Thursday-Friday at the 84 Lumber to finish dead last.

Two September golf tournaments that she could easily have skipped.

A combined 29 strokes over par.

Michelle Wie turned 17 on October 11, the day before the 2006 Samsung World Championship began at the Bighorn Golf Club in Palm Desert, California, near her family's second home. The year before, days after she turned professional, her Samsung galleries were jam-packed. Now, only a few people followed her around the Bighorn course during her appearance in the pro-am.

"I think I'm invincible," Wie said when asked afterward about her brutal schedule. "I think I can play every week. But I'm still human."

Human enough to build a snowman, the dreaded but all too familiar figure on the scorecards of weekend hackers around the world. On the first day, her drive on 14 came to rest nestled against a small rock, and she asked for a free drop. She got the ruling and dropped her ball into the desert, behind a small tree. Then the wind, which had been holding back the branches, eased. Suddenly she couldn't see the fairway. She waited for the next gust, hurried to hit, and missed the ball completely. Then she pitched into a thicket and had to take an unplayable. The next shot came from a cart path, and that proved costliest of all, as she jammed her right wrist hard against the path on the downswing. Wie took a half hour to build her quadruple-bogey 8, an ordeal that delayed the entire round so much that the players behind her took nearly five hours to finish, even though they were two to a group. Karrie Webb called the wait "ridiculous."

Wie shot a 74 that day, an eagle partially offsetting the snowman. The next three rounds—72, 72, 75—added up to 5-

over for the tournament, 21 strokes behind winner Lorena Ochoa. Wie finished 17th in a field of 20.

But far worse than her score was her wrist injury, which almost no one in Palm Desert—or anywhere else—even knew she had.

Before Samsung, Wie had acknowledged that "I have to learn how to schedule better, how much my body can take and when I should play. My first year, I haven't got it down yet. Obviously, I learn from my mistakes."

Maybe not. Team Wie next flew 5,400 miles west to Kochi, Japan, so that Michelle could tee it up for the second time at the Casio World Open. She should have stayed at home: nine bogeys on Thursday (81), six more plus a double on Friday (80), no birdies. She edged Japanese amateur Tomomichi Oto (161 to 162) to finish next to last, 17 strokes over par.

Counting Casio, in her last four men's tournaments of the 2006 season Michelle Wie finished a combined 46 strokes over par in three, with a WD in the fourth.

The Wies flew in a therapist named Jay Kiss, who works with Paul Gagné in Montreal, to look at Michelle's right wrist. Kiss saw trouble right away in the ligaments that connected the two forearm bones, the radius and the ulna: "She injured a couple of the collateral ligaments on the ulnar side. It was a sprain. And she had adhesions through the extensor tendons. When she went into flexion, a sheet of tissue was getting caught, not latching on."

Translation: Michelle had a condition that triggered major pain whenever she rolled her wrist, which was every time she swung a golf club.

Kiss took an hour to "reposition the bones," employing

what he calls "a mixed martial arts of therapy." Wie felt better the next day. Kiss also noticed "torsion in her pelvis"— probably the pain that caused her first visit to the medical tent before the John Deere Classic. A 17-year-old golfer with a medical chart worthy of a football player.

Wie showed up in January at Waialae for the 2007 Sony Open with a bandage on her right wrist. She called it a "little injury," and said she wasn't sure exactly what it was, even though Kiss had diagnosed it for her.

The year before, her first hole featured a gridlock of journalists, fans, and other players stopping to watch her tee off. This time, a fan held up a sign that read, "Wie??? Why!!!" Wie herself admitted later that she found herself wondering, "Why am I doing this?" She hit two bunkers, two water hazards, and two palm trees before hitting her first fairway. She shot 78 on her home course, and then finished her two-day tournament the next day with a 76 to miss the cut by 14 strokes.

The bright spot of the winter came at the Punahou computer lab. Wie dragged two friends to a terminal and followed instructions on how to find out if she got admitted early to Stanford. Wie typed in the information, and the three friends screamed in joy: *She got in!*

On February 9, 2007, Jesse Derris of Ken Sunshine Consultants issued a statement:

FOR IMMEDIATE RELEASE
MICHELLE WIE INJURES WRIST

HONOLULU—Michelle Wie injured her wrist in an accidental fall while running earlier this week, and has had the injury set in a hard cast to facilitate her recovery. Her doctor expects it will take four to six weeks to heal.

Michelle's playing schedule will be altered as needed to allow the injury to fully heal.

The first alteration took place immediately: Wie announced that she was withdrawing from the Kraft Nabisco Championship, the LPGA Tour's premier showcase, where she'd had one of her three Top-5 finishes in majors the year before.

That was major news, but there were no further details forthcoming from her public relations agency or the Wies. No mention of the location or even the nature of the injury. Was it a fracture? A sprain? Where was she running? In Honolulu? In California? Who was her doctor? And, the most basic question of all, which wrist was it?

Reports at the time said it was her left wrist. Michelle had been questioned about rolling her left wrist back in March, during a press conference before the Kraft Nabisco. She stung the same left wrist on a downswing on the ninth hole of the first round of the 2006 Women's U.S. Open. But the month before, she had showed up at the Sony Open with her right wrist bandaged. That was the wrist she had hurt on a cart path mishap in late 2006. Then a report in a Honolulu paper said she fell on her left wrist.

Left? Right? Maybe it didn't matter: her trainer, Paul Gagné, said Wie had had problems with both wrists dating back three years.

The vagueness of the statement and the secretiveness of Team Wie set media tongues to wagging. One critic claimed that the 17-year-old was "totally dispirited by her poor finishes among the men in the second half of 2006" and that this was the cause of her withdrawal from the Kraft Nabisco, not her wrist. Others sniped that "Michelle Wie the Phenom" had become yesterday's news, that the arrogance and aloofness of Team Wie had gotten just plain tiresome. All seemed to forget or discount the extraordinary performance of a teenager in women's majors over the last two years. Instead, the golf media focused on what Michelle Wie had *not* done—live up to the impossibly high expectations she had created for herself, and which her adoring public shared.

Now, with her swing in shambles, her wrists injured, and her confidence nowhere in sight, those expectations were plummeting to earth.

"The question of 'when,' " the AP's Doug Ferguson wrote, "is slowly shifting to 'if.' "

Free Fall

Michelle Wie was ready to play golf again.

After four months on the shelf, she'd been cleared by doctors at Kaiser Permanente, the health care provider the Wies used in Hawaii, to pick up her driver again. She was good to go.

Family and friends gathered at a house on Ko Olina in May 2007 to celebrate her green light—and her impending graduation from high school—with lots of food and laughter. Michelle's classmates had lobbied hard for her to make it to graduation, but on that weekend Michelle would be in Mt. Pleasant, South Carolina, playing in the Ginn Tribute Hosted by Annika Sorenstam, a tournament making its debut on the LPGA circuit. The best Michelle could do was provide a life-sized picture of herself mounted on poster board as a stand-in.

The layoff had been an ordeal. She loved her friends, and she did go to her senior prom in a limo with a big group, but everyone understood how much she wanted to return to the golf course. So the mood at the party was exuberant, as if the worst were over, even though soon Michelle would once again be a part-timer in her own hometown.

Wie hadn't practiced much during her rehab. Her accuracy wasn't all that sharp. Her distance didn't make any jaws drop. No one, including the Wies themselves, could really know if Michelle was coming back too soon. But eagerness overwhelmed all worry, as always. In a story about the Ginn Tribute and Michelle's comeback in the *Honolulu Advertiser,* Greg Nichols, the pro at Ko Olina Golf Club, said that the opening 18 on May 31 would be "the most important round of golf in her life."

Wie played her Tuesday practice round at the RiverTowne Country Club wearing dark sunglasses and a floppy white hat pulled down over her forehead. Afterward, at a press conference, Michelle looked content on the podium, with her eyes wide and her face tanned. "I never realized how much I missed it," she said. "How much I actually love golf, how much I love being out here at tournaments. So I'm just so grateful that my wrist is better, and I can actually hit a golf ball and be at this tournament and play this week."

But then specific questions about her injured wrist started up hot and heavy, and so did the confusion.

Asked when she started practicing again: "I forget."

Asked if she's pain-free: "Yeah. Relatively. There's mostly no pain. But once in a while, when I hit a bad shot, there's a little zinger here and there, but mostly it's been feeling really great."

Asked the extent of the injuries: "Well, I mean, I don't really want to go back into the past and talk about the injuries. I don't really want to go into the details of it. Both wrists have bothered me for a while. It's all better now, and I don't think that talking about the injury will help me or anyone."

The next day, a column in the local paper was entitled "Michelle Wie: A Study in Celebrity vs. Credibility."

What was she hiding?

Flashback to January 23, 2007, when Wendy Howard met Michelle Wie, only days before she injured her left wrist in a fall while running.

They met in the Honolulu office of Dr. Milton Kurashige, who worked for Body Balance for Performance, and who had not been able to figure out why Michelle's right wrist, the one that had been bothering her since the previous October, wasn't healing. He called for a backup consultation with Howard, a physical-occupational therapist who specialized in hands.

Born and raised in Honolulu, Howard got her occupational therapy degree at San Jose State in 1993 and then went on to a five-year program at Stanford in which she specialized in hand injuries. She returned to Hawaii in 2003 and started her own practice and research on wrist fractures.

Howard became particularly fascinated with a little-studied ligament-cartilage structure called the triangular fibrocartilage complex, which was introduced to the medical community in 1981. "It's an unusual ligament," she explains, "and it's essential for grip." The triangular-shaped ligament with its cartilage cushion connects the two major forearm bones, the radius and the ulna, and the ulnar carpus. Put simply, the strength of the TFCC allows grip and the shape allows rotation. Think of a three-sided rubber band stabilizing the wrist.

Howard has seen hundreds of patients, many of them golfers, and nearly all of them walked into her office with their hand clenched around their injured wrist as if trying to keep their two forearm bones together with a clamp. She believed they all suffered from the same thing: a weakened TFCC. So she asked one of them who was a seamstress to fabricate a brace. The seamstress put together some cloth and Velcro and strapped it on. Weeks later, the seamstress' pain was gone. Howard asked for more braces, which she then gave to more patients, only to hear the same success stories, over and over. Patients called—guitarists, surfers, golfers—to rave. She said she felt like she'd landed in an infomercial.

One of the first steps Howard took was to measure Wie's grip strength. She had Michelle squeeze a device called a dynamometer with her injured right hand. The meter read 60 pounds, normal for an adult woman. Then Howard told Wie to switch hands. This time the meter registered 120 pounds. The machine must be broken, Howard thought. She asked Kurashige for another dynamometer and measured again. And again: 120 pounds. Wie was off the charts.

Howard asked Wie where it hurt. Michelle pointed to several spots on her right hand, her wrist, even her elbow and shoulder. Howard asked when the pain had begun. Almost exactly two years before, when she was 15, Wie said. Some days it was better, others worse. Howard's mind raced. She figured teenage hormones were aggravating the issue. She wondered about repeated stress. "What's the longest you've gone without swinging a club?" Howard asked.

Wie said, "Two weeks."

Howard asked for the date of her last X-rays. Wie said she'd not had any X-rays taken. What about an MRI? No, no MRI either. Howard asked if she could call the family doctor; Michelle said she didn't remember his name. Howard looked over at Bo; she couldn't remember either.

"I'm thinking, *You gotta be kidding me,*" Howard said later. "They're sitting on $50 million. What am I missing here? Maybe they're afraid of talking about it."

One symptom didn't fit. Wie spoke of a shooting pain in

the knuckle of her right index finger, and said that she had had acupuncture. Howard believes in acupuncture but wondered where the specialist had inserted the needles. Wie pointed to the base of her thumb. Howard sighed. The acupuncturist had struck a nerve, she concluded, and that was what was causing all the pain.

The meeting lasted more than an hour. Howard told Michelle and her mother that Michelle had a very serious injury. She told Wie that she must take some time off and spend it healing. Wie didn't respond. Neither did Bo. They parted without even a word of thanks. Obviously Howard's prescription—time away from golf—was unacceptable to Team Wie.

Howard saw Michelle again a few weeks later. This time, she brought along a WristWidget, a small brace that looks a little bit like a guard used by in-line skaters, and she fitted it around Michelle's right wrist. Then Howard brought out the dynamometer. This time the meter read 120 pounds. She looked up at Wie's face. There was no reaction.

"I really think," Howard said shortly after this encounter, "she's a beaten-down soul."

Michelle Wie teed it up for the first time since January's bombout at the Sony Classic on a hot South Carolina morning on the last day of May. Her playing partners were Alena Sharp and Janice Moodie. The round would be the strangest of Wie's career.

The most ominous sign came first, as Wie emerged at the 10th tee (the group's first hole) to see only a couple of dozen people in the stands. The year before, fans had lined up six deep at tournaments just to catch a glimpse of her. Now she was simply "Next on the tee, from Honolulu, Michelle Wie."

She parred the first hole, a good sign. But that was the last one of the day. She found water on the second hole: bogey. Next, she snap-hooked her tee shot into the woods and made double bogey. And it didn't get any better.

"She didn't look like she was there," Sharp said later. "She didn't focus like usual." Sharp thought Wie would withdraw after nine holes; Wie later said she should have.

Another bogey after finding a bunker on the fourth hole. Murmurs went through the small gallery. She looked listless and cramped. One Asian reporter speculated loudly about how much weight she had gained.

Then came a bizarre scene. She blocked her drive on the par-3 15th into the trees and walked to find her ball. Another new caddy, David Clark, helped, as did B.J. and Bo and Linda Johnston, one of her "aunties" who frequently made trips to see Michelle play. No luck. Michelle announced her intent to take an unplayable lie. Then B.J. said something to Clark: "What about the tee?" Michelle immediately announced she was going back to the tee. She told her partners to putt out; she was going to hit again from the tee.

Moodie cautioned B.J. about Rule 8–1, which forbids a player from soliciting advice. "During a stipulated round," the rule reads, "a player must not . . . ask for advice from anyone other than his partner or either of their caddies." The penalty was two strokes. After Wie blocked her second shot and ended up with a triple bogey, B.J. approached rules official Angus McKenzie and spoke with him for several minutes while his daughter moved to the next hole. McKenzie said later that B.J. Wie had an explanation for the interaction, saying he was only asking the caddy, "What are the options?" But more than one person present heard B.J. utter the word *tee*. And they also heard Clark's response: "It's three from the tee."

Technically, Wie did not break any rules. She did not actively ask for help. But McKenzie told B.J., "When in doubt, don't." Minutes later, after B.J. left, McKenzie heard the reporters' version of the events and said: "It's all based on integrity. Somebody's gonna sleep tonight. Somebody's not."

Later on, Commissioner Carolyn Bivens insisted: "There was no rules violation." But not many who heard the story cared for the technicality. B.J. Wie was at it again, feeding the worst concerns, controlling his daughter.

"Anybody can say something from outside the ropes," Sharp said later. "But he was too close. He's always so close to her. You're going to get your daughter in trouble. Everyone at the range was talking about it."

Wie went limp. She sighed repeatedly. She showed little energy, trudging along to her ball and taking less than the usual time lining up putts. She said almost nothing to her playing partners or to her caddy. And no wonder. Her round felt like a geological excursion, going from water to pavement to sand to tall grass. She was 8 over after seven holes.

Things only got weirder on the second nine. On the par-5 3rd hole, Bivens suddenly appeared on the fringe of the fairway. She rarely showed up on the course during play, and yet there she was, speaking with rules officials. Wie's tee shot veered out of bounds, into a street, off a car, and down a storm drain. Bivens stood by as a little boy got on his hands and knees to peer into the drain in search of the ball. Wie played a provisional and hooked that into a pond. She walked toward the street in hopes of finding her ball, then turned and retraced her steps to the tee for the second time in the round. She eventually carded a quintuple-bogey 10.

Now she was 12 over after 12 holes.

In the media tent, LPGA officials began discussing the obscure "Rule of 88," which states that a nonmember who shoots 88 must withdraw and is subsequently banned from LPGA cosponsored events for the remainder of the calendar season. Wie was now in jeopardy of getting booted for the rest of 2007. But the rule never crossed Wie's mind. Probably she'd never heard of it, and if she had, she couldn't in her worst nightmares have thought that it might ever have to be invoked against her.

Suddenly, William Morris rep Greg Nared had a cell phone to his ear. This was out of the ordinary: normally, Nared never took his eyes off Wie and never took calls on the course. Yet now he swiveled away from the ropes and covered his mouth as he spoke into his flip phone.

Soon Nared began talking with B.J. Wie. Chris Higgs, the LPGA chief operations officer, drove up in a cart and spoke with Nared. This was rare, too: Higgs rarely showed up on the course. Now both he and Bivens appeared within minutes of each other, along with a clutter of rules officials in red jackets. Asked why he came out, Higgs told a reporter, "For no particular reason."

Wie's score climbed to 14-over, two strokes from banishment for the season. Nared approached her after she finished up on the seventh hole. They spoke briefly. Moments later, Wie announced to her playing partners that she was withdrawing from the tournament because of her wrist.

Nared explained later that he knew of Wie's injury, and that Wie told him at the rope that she aggravated her wrist, but he never explained why he waited so long to approach her. Either way, Wie had a 43 on the front and a 7-over 35 on the back—through seven holes. She shook hands with her competitors, glumly climbed into a cart, and rode to the clubhouse, where she met behind closed doors with her parents and Nared. The four spoke for 15 minutes, then an ice pack was brought in for Wie's left wrist, the wrist she hurt in the fall. Wie then walked to the media tent without the ice pack.

An LPGA PR rep spoon-fed Wie her first answer: "Michelle,

thank you for coming in after your withdrawal from the tournament because of your wrist. Are you optimistic from here on out once your wrist does heal?"

Wie said, "It felt good when I was practicing, but I kind of tweaked it in the middle of the round a little bit. So I'm just taking cautionary measures, and I know what to work on. The only way to go from here is up, so I'm feeling pretty good about it."

Wie did not look like she was feeling good about anything.

She elaborated: "Well, I think that when an injury is in the back of your mind, you're thinking, 'Oh, this is going to hurt.' The last thing you're thinking about is trying to hit the ball straight."

Few in the pressroom bought that.

Neither did Alena Sharp, who'd been playing alongside Wie through the whole nightmare. "She wasn't holding her wrist," Sharp said, when told later of Michelle's explanation to the media. "I think she just had a bad day. If it was her wrist, why wait until the last two holes to withdraw?"

"I kind of felt bad for her," Sharp added. "She didn't seem happy."

Two days after Ken Sunshine rep Jesse Derris declared that Wie's status for the LPGA Championship was "100 percent up in the air," Michelle was at Bulle Rock Golf Club in Havre de Grace, Maryland, pounding golf balls on the range.

Wie did have a chronic injury, one that only caused sharp pain at certain times. But the sight of her whipping her wrists through an array of shots convinced a lot of LPGA players and media hounds that she must have faked the pain down in South Carolina to avoid getting barred from LPGA tournaments for the rest of the season.

Not only was she practicing just 48 hours after her WD for medical reasons, but she was also taking advantage of her nonmember status to gain access to the course before Sunday at 5:00 p.m., the earliest Tour members are allowed on to practice prior to a tournament. This was just seven days after LPGA Tour players met with officials to complain about Wie practicing too early at the Ginn Tribute course. So a lot of golf people grumbled that Wie was both skirting the rules (dodging the Rule of 88 by feigning an injury) *and* exploiting them (practicing before any of her competitors could).

Fallout came from an unexpected source: Annika Sorenstam, one of the least outspoken superstars in the golf galaxy (or any other, for that matter). She hosted the Ginn tournament, and when asked at the LPGA Championship about Wie's withdrawal, she cut loose:

> I just feel that there's a little bit of lack of respect and class just to kind of leave a tournament like that and then come out and practice here. . . . I don't know the situation, if it's injury or whatever it is. It just seemed really weird. . . . I know what it's like to be injured. I mean, when I was injured, I wasn't able to touch golf clubs for weeks. It's a little funny that you pull out with an injury and then you start grinding. My doctor told me to rest.

Asked whether she thought Wie quit because of the Rule of 88 or the wrist, Sorenstam said, "I have no idea what it is, but I know that . . . when you get a sponsor invitation, I think you have some responsibilities to the sponsor, to the organizer, and I can tell you that from being part of it now, it's a different side from that aspect."

That same day, Rick Maese of the *Baltimore Sun* reported on Wie's LPGA Championship Pro-Am, saying she needed treatment during the round not on her left wrist, which was iced after the withdrawal from Ginn, but on her right wrist.

Not only that, Maese continued, she needed a refresher course in Golf Etiquette 101: "On the second-to-last hole, she actually plopped herself onto the grass, while waiting her turn to hit. She sat cross-legged in the middle of the fairway, fingering one of the dolls that dangled from her golf bag. For a moment, she didn't seem to notice that her back was turned to one of her playing partners, who stood just a few feet away and was addressing his ball."

That scene intensified the long-held feeling that Wie simply didn't appreciate anyone outside her circle. So did the news that Commissioner Bivens met with the Wies to relay criticism of Michelle's attitude during the Pro-Am. And the lack of information on her wrist injury—some players and reporters simply didn't believe she even had a wrist injury—only made things worse.

Even Lily Yao, one of Michelle's greatest supporters outside her family, didn't get it. "When she injured her wrist at Samsung," she said, "nobody knew. When she played badly at Casio, then the news of her wrist came out. When you are injured, any part of your body, you better heal. I understand the anxiety to get back out there, but they didn't tell anybody she hurt it, and she continued to play. That's when I begin to wonder, 'Why?' "

At her own press conference, Wie tried to clarify:

The reason why I withdrew last week was because of my left wrist.... I should have stopped playing when I tweaked it on the 10th hole. But, you know, as stubborn as I am, I just kept on playing.... If I played those last two holes, I don't think I would be here today playing this week.

At first when I hurt my wrist, I didn't really know what was going on. So I didn't want to tell the media ... Now I'm completely sure and I'm fine with telling about my injury and telling what went wrong. ... I was in California at my aunt's house, and just thought it would be good to work out. I was like, I haven't worked out in a couple of days. ... And I was running, which is quite stupid; people that know me, [they know] I can't run at all ... and I fell over something, it was about 6:30 in the morning and my brain doesn't function. ... I was like, okay, just a little sore, it's a little swollen. [And then it was] oh, I can't move it anymore, what's going on ... There was a lot of conflicting information between those couple of months. So I didn't really want to release anything.

Sorenstam's criticism? Unwarranted: "I mean, well, you know, just I don't think I need to apologize for anything."

Her interaction with Pro-Am partners at the LPGA? "I think it was very insulting because I tried my best. It was my sixth year out here already and I played in numerous pro-ams and I think it's ridiculous to make any false accusations about me. ... I have way too many other things to think about. I have housing applications [at Stanford] to do this week. I have way too many other things to stress about."

The press conference only made matters worse.

- She said she fell over "something," but that only added to the confusion.
- She said more practice and tournament play would make the wrist stronger, but she withdrew from Ginn because of her wrist, and said, "I can, you know, hypothetically, hurt it again."

- She took a sponsor's exemption for a tournament, withdrew from it, and still, "I don't think I need to apologize for anything."
- And when some of the biggest contributors to the tournaments—those invited to play in Pro-Ams—complained about her attitude enough to get the LPGA Tour commissioner upset, Wie called the accusations "insulting" and "false," then said she didn't "really know the full story myself," and added that she had "way too many other things to stress about."

All of Wie's problems, from years in the past, finally caught up to her.

"She's no longer the prodigy that amazed the golf world with such power for such youth," wrote the AP's Doug Ferguson. "She is 17, but no longer a kid. There was a time the LPGA Tour needed Wie a lot more than Wie needed the LPGA Tour. That might not be the case anymore. People are far more willing to forgive a bad round than bad manners."

Team Wie had no obvious goals other than to keep Michelle out on the course, no matter what the risks. As a consequence, her wrist pain, ignored and endured for two full years, had not only ruined her game but also had angered almost everyone because she hadn't been forthcoming with clear, solid information about its extent.

Michelle Wie could now tell the whole truth and nothing but the truth, only to be doubted. She had gone from incredible to credible to uncredible.

Some of the blame for Wie's physical problems was directed at David Leadbetter, as members of the media began to whisper about "Lead poisoning." Leadbetter admitted that Wie had lost upper-body and hand strength, and the new imbalance with her still-strong legs had distorted her swing and caused accuracy problems. He laid some blame on the mats at the practice range at Waialae, saying Wie had complained to him about how they stung her wrists.

"She never allowed her wrist to really heal," Leadbetter said. "The verdict is still out on how much a kid should practice. . . . Kids can pick up an injury unless it's monitored. I've warned her. Practice doesn't always make perfect. She's practicing smarter now. But because she's such a competitor, that sometimes overrides logic."

Wie's easy swing had become as forced as her smile. Was that because of her injury? Because of her added muscle mass? Because of a lack of confidence? Because of Leadbetter's tinkering? All of the above? In a way, it didn't matter, because she started leaving her driver in the bag.

Gone was the achingly beautiful arc that made her special and rescued her from trouble both on and off the course.

Gone also were the personality, the playfulness, the innocence of a child thrilled to be doing well in an adult's world.

Gone was the jokester, the ham, the delightful young woman who now lived only on her school campus, and maybe in her heart.

The LPGA Championship was another disaster.

She finished last, all alone in 84th place, the only player to take more than 300 strokes in four rounds. A new physical therapist B.J. Wie had hired walked the ropes and occasionally darted onto the course to massage one or both of Michelle's wrists. Wie concealed external signs of her pain, so many observers thought she was embellishing or making excuses or simply lying. "If she misses this putt," one reporter commented after an on-course rehab session, "her wrist is really going to start hurting."

Loehr always encouraged Wie to tell herself a story of her improvement: each stumbling block is a passageway, a plot twist, on the way to a happy ending. Each missed putt clears the way for made putts later. But he always gave Wie a caveat: the story must be nonfiction. "It has to be a story that is grounded in truth," he said. "Face the truth, and make sure whatever story she creates is grounded in reality and takes her where she wants to go."

Near the end of 2007, Loehr stopped working with the Wies.

Wie went to North Carolina for the U.S. Women's Open, and shot 82 on the first day. "It's shocking," she said to reporters afterward, "because . . . I know I played better than this. It's just a very fine line between shooting 69 and shooting what I shot today."

The next day, she withdrew, citing wrist pain.

Some speculated that Sony and Nike were forcing Michelle Wie to play. Not so, they said. "We want Michelle to perform and do the best she can," said Sony senior consultant Mike Dyer. "Nobody wants to push her to play before she's ready. From a Sony perspective, the bottom line is there is no one pushing her. We need her to be successful and to be successful she needs to do the things to get her game on track."

Team Wie didn't even listen to the people who lined their pockets.

"When I last saw her," Lily Yao said in July 2007, "I said, 'Make sure you are 100 percent recovered before you pick up a golf club.' She said 'I will, I will.' It's a case of poor management by the team. She was temporarily burned out. Get your mind fresh and clear and then come back. But they continue to play and pull themselves down."

Wie did skip the John Deere Classic because of her wrists, but then she flew to Europe for the high-purse Evian Masters, where once again she took more than 300 strokes in four rounds. Then she continued to St. Andrews in Scotland for the British Open, where B.J. Wie admitted to the press, "We were a bit naive" about the speed of Michelle's recovery. She shot 73–80 to miss an LPGA cut for the first time since she was 13 years old.

Back on that day, August 15, 2003, 13-year-old Michelle Wie had spoken to a few reporters in a greenside interview after her final hole on Friday at the State Farm Classic in Springfield, Illinois. Clearly exhausted from a long summer, she confessed that she just wanted to go home. "No," said B.J. Wie, interrupting his daughter. "We're going to the range."

Four years later, the girl whose dream was to live outside of the box had become trapped in one.

The Next ... Who?

The man who never sat down on a golf course while his daughter was playing was now sitting down on almost every hole. B.J. Wie walked up each fairway at the LPGA qualifying school in Daytona in the first week of December 2008, placed his backpack on the ground by the green, and rested as he waited for his daughter to make her way toward the flag. He greeted media and fans with more than the usual politeness, even warmness. His wife, Bo, smiled often, another rarity. The couple even shared a hug after their daughter shot a blistering 65 in the second round of the five-round event.

The earth had shifted since Michelle Wie went into free fall in mid-2006. The public relations firm hired back then to handle her impending superstardom no longer posted a rep to keep track of her every public move. The William Morris Agency would be replaced within months by IMG. No Nike or Sony employee walked the course to monitor the $10,000,000 investment they'd made in "the next Tiger Woods" three years before. Perhaps most telling, there wasn't a live television camera to be found.

Swing-coach-to-the-stars David Leadbetter did accompany Michelle on her five-round odyssey, and he admitted, for the first time, the extent of Michelle's injuries, saying that he had spent the past year working around her left wrist instead of just resting it. "Her left side was so weak it was hard for her to hold onto the club," he said. "It never came down in the same plane at the same time." The result: a significant loss in power brought on by a seriously out-of-kilter swing.

"You're at the peak of Mt. Everest one day and then you're down in the dumps," Leadbetter said as he walked toward the 18th tee on the LPGA International Champions Course on a chilly Sunday afternoon. "She's doing it now because she wants to do it. Not because she's being told."

There were signs of a new maturity in the Stanford sophomore. She took fewer risks with her driver, rarely went for par 5 greens in two, and bounced back from missed chances better than the riverboat gambler who had formerly controlled her golf psyche. The result: scores of 69, 65, 72, 68, 74 to finish T-12 in a grueling event in which the top 20 finishers earned fully exempt status on the 2009 LPGA Tour.

After nearly a decade in the spotlight, Michelle Wie still had a chance to conquer and captivate.

The year leading up to Michelle Wie's enrollment in Q-school had been nothing short of awful. After making the *Forbes* list of Top 20 Earners Under 25 in December 2007, with an annual income of $19,000,000 and change, she learned she would not get a sponsor's exemption to her hometown Sony Open in January 2008. At the Fields Open at Ko Olina in February, she finished 72nd, last among all players who had made the cut.

Wie received a sponsor's invitation to the Safeway International the following month, but pulled out with another aggravation of her left wrist injury. She missed the cut at the Michelob Ultra Open, and then failed to qualify for the 2008 U.S. Women's Open.

The avalanche that began in the late summer of 2006 had only gained speed.

Her fortune seemed to turn at the State Farm Classic in July, as the old Michelle Wie showed up and shot 17-under through three rounds, only one stroke off the lead. Then disaster: Wie somehow failed to sign her second-round scorecard and was disqualified.

After 53 sponsor's exemptions or invitations in 62 LPGA tournaments since 2001, Wie found herself with nowhere to play. Men's events had enough of her unsightly scores and quick exits. Women's events wouldn't keep inviting her while everyone else had to qualify. She averaged a 76.7 in 2008 and broke 70 exactly zero times.

So her decision to go to the 2008 LPGA qualifying school was an easy one.

She had no other choice.

What happened to the Big Wiesy, the captivating teenager who was destined—Arnold Palmer said it all the way back in 2003— "to influence the golfing scene as much as Tiger, maybe more?"

What happened to the Sure Thing?

HER SWING DESERTED HER ...

The perfect, and perfectly repeatable, swing that sent her drives and irons far and straight every time, that put her in contention to win any women's event, vanished in the summer of

2006, only to be replaced by a robotic motion bearing scant resemblance to the original.

Maybe it was David Leadbetter's tinkering.

Maybe it was her parents' incessant hovering.

Maybe it was the injuries.

Maybe it was all of the above.

But once the great swing vanished, Michelle Wie's name vanished from leader boards.

HER PUTTING WENT FROM MEDIOCRE TO POOR . . .

Few golfers excel at putting as teens, but Team Wie made the learning curve steeper by skipping junior tournaments altogether and jumping from men's events to women's events and back again—sometimes in the same week.

No truism in golf is truer than "Drive for show, putt for dough." If you can't sink enough six-footers to save par, it doesn't matter how many 300-yard drives you hit.

HER BODY GAVE OUT UNDER THE PHYSICAL STRESS . . .

Most professional golfers live within a five-hour flight of the majority of their tournaments. (Michelle, remember, grew up in Hawaii.) Most pro golfers don't go to school full-time. Most pro golfers aren't teenagers. Most pro golfers don't have to deal with more than a few commercial appearances per season. And, of course, most pro golfers play on only one tour.

Michelle Wie fit into none of these categories. Her parents had to have seen the evidence of her exhaustion even before Michelle turned pro, but they did nothing to adjust to what was happening to her. They didn't move (at least for the golf season) to the mainland. They didn't homeschool their daughter. They didn't ease Michelle into endorsements and business deals.

And they didn't rethink their approach even when Michelle began to break down from illness and injury.

The root cause of her decline, the force that contributed to all the factors that brought her down, was greed.

Team Wie—make that B.J. and Bo Wie, with Michelle playing the role of money machine—clearly felt they could have it all: the riches, the fame, and the celebrity lifestyle. They felt they could accomplish that by having their daughter do it all: the LPGA Tour, the PGA Tour, the international events, the promotional appearances for sponsors looking to wring every last dollar out of her. And they felt they could master it all: the right way to schedule, the right way to swing, the right way to read greens, and even the right way to heal.

So many of Michelle Wie's struggles could have been eased or eliminated if her parents had been less controlling, less impatient, less aggressive—and less greedy. With more downtime, Michelle could have healed quicker and focused better. She almost certainly could have learned to be a better putter with more reliance on professional instructors—and far less on B.J.'s tutelage and charting of greens. She could have had more physical stamina in reserve had her parents set up household on the mainland. She could undoubtedly have learned to finish tournaments better with more experience in junior tournaments.

But all that's blood under the bridge.

What's next for Michelle Wie?

That's up to her, but be assured that the Michelle Wie story is far from over. She still powers her driver nearly 300 yards. She still commands the biggest galleries and the most media attention every time she tees it up. Now, armed with her LPGA Tour card, Michelle Wie has a chance to seize control of her golf and her life.

She has time.

Annika Sorenstram didn't win her first LPGA tournament until she was 24.

Michelle Wie doesn't turn 20 until October 2009.

This book begins with Michelle Wie, then just 10 years old, bubbling enthusiastically about her love of golf and about her dream of playing on the PGA Tour, and about her favorite golfer in the world, Tiger Woods: "I think I can beat him in the near future. Like when I'm 15."

So let's end it by hearing directly from her again, this time shortly after she won her 2009 LPGA Tour card:

Getting my card is a big triumph for me. I'm really proud of myself. There were times in the past couple of years, with all the injuries and the stress, when I was so tired all the time. I took four or five naps during the day. All I wanted to do was sleep.

But this is a new beginning. I feel so much more energized now.

Even before I broke my wrist in early 2007, my whole right side was really hurting from when I hit a cart path on my downswing in my first year as a pro. I would compensate with my shoulder, elbow, neck, everything. One thing led to another, and it affected my whole swing.

Then I fell while working out, and I didn't tell my parents. I fell on my butt, and I thought it was a tailbone injury. I thought I'd have a huge bruise. But then I saw my wrist was twisted in a weird way. The more I moved it, the more it hurt. I just hid it in my sleeve. I didn't want my parents to worry about me, because when they worry, I worry. Turns out I broke three bones. My parents were

shocked when I told them. I needed a cast, and to be honest, I wanted to put my whole body in a cast.

I was in a pretend world. I didn't want to face reality.
I wanted to act like everything was okay. The more I
played, the more it hurt. The worse I played, the more I
tried to practice. It was a never-ending cycle. I thought
everything would be fine once I got my cast off, but then
I did and my left arm had shrunk. I'd hit a couple balls,
and I needed to get the cast back on. I would cry, then get
frustrated at myself for crying, and then I'd cry some
more. It got to the point where I couldn't lift a golf club
at all.

There were times when I was like, "Is this really all
worth it?" But when you hit that one good shot, it reminds you why you play the game. I wanted to taste that
again.

I've learned to respect my body. I'm eating better, trying to keep my body toxin-free. And I'm getting there.
Pain-wise, I'm almost all better. I'm not scared all the time
of something hurting when I swing. The hardest part is
getting rid of all the compensation. Because of the pain,
there were little things I did to protect my swing. I'm still
trying to iron those out.

And there's another thing I'm working on. I know
some people in the media want me to play like I did at 14.
For a while, I did, too. But I started realizing you can
never be who you were five years ago. You can only move
forward and become more mature. I think my parents
have realized that, too.

Everyone was really stressed out for a while. I think
we all needed to take a chill pill.

Stanford helps with that. My schedule is great. All
my classes are in the morning, when it can get pretty cold

up in Palo Alto. Every afternoon, though, the weather's perfect, so I practice until it gets dark. After that, I do some homework. It's a good balance. I can't just be playing golf. I need something else in my life. I live with other athletes, and they call me "a civilian." I like that.

School really calms me. Yes, I might have to sacrifice some good grades. But it's a great time in my life right now.

And yes, I do want to play against men again. Definitely. It's always been my dream, and I'm not giving it up. But for now, I just want to try to be the number one woman golfer in the world.

I'm really excited now. And I'm so excited to feel excited again. I think it's going to be a great time ahead.

I'm finally happy.

ACKNOWLEDGMENTS

● ●

Thanks first and foremost to the Wie family for the time they gave me for this project. And especially, thanks to Michelle, for her courage.

A lot of people on Team Wie put up with a lot of pestering from me, notably Ross Berlin, Jesse Derris, Paul Gagne, Gary Gilchrist, Greg Johnston, David Leadbetter, Greg Nared, and Jill Smoller. My sincere thanks to them.

This book would never have happened without Greg Dinkin and Frank Scatoni at Venture Literary, who believed in it from the very beginning, and Gary Hoenig at ESPN Publishing, who backed it. My manager, Sherman Brown, and ESPN's Geoff Reiss and Keith Clinkscales all helped in crucial ways. So did Steve Wulf, Sandy DeShong, and John Glenn of ESPN Books and Paul Taunton of Ballantine Books.

My editors—Michael Solomon, Christian Wright, Chris Raymond, and Glen Waggoner—all made this book better while dealing with me at my worst. I also want to thank my editors at *ESPN The Magazine,* who supported me even though it meant less time for my job. And I want to salute three generations of golf editors at ESPN.com—David Lefort, Jason Sobel, and Kevin Maguire—for being so incredibly easy to work with and so very good at their jobs.

Many sources in Hawaii offered great aloha spirit, most of all Del-Marc Fujita, Wendy Howard, Casey Nakama, and Lily Yao.

I deeply appreciate those in the golf-writing community who took time to help me stay out of the rough even as they did their own assignments. Among them (alphabetically): Beth Ann Baldry, Damon Hack, Bob Harig, Sean Lunasco, Jim McCabe, Dave Reardon, Adam Schupak, and Michael Won. But I must add that no one helped me more than Ron Sirak and Doug Ferguson, both of whom make me proud to be a journalist.

The LPGA staff was amazing from the beginning. Thanks to Ty Votaw, Dana Gordon, Terumi Kaibara, Laura Neal, Dana Gross-Rhode, Kyumin Shim, and—especially—Paul Rovnak.

Many friends encouraged me and kept my spirits up even when it seemed this book might never happen: Dwayne Albert, Amanda Angel, Lindsay Berra, Bobby Conroy, Jim Darlington, Jamey Eisenberg, Bruce Feldman, Mark Giles, Chris Glew, Jemele Hill, Lynn Hoppes, Melissa Jacobs, Dave and Sara Koch, Jamian Lai, Alex Lin, Jay Lovinger, Rick Maese, Mike Rosenberg, Darren Rovell, Alyssa Roenigk, Mary Sadanaga, Pete Thamel, Max Thompson, Wright Thompson, and Seth Wickersham.

Thanks also to a group of Michigan alums who kept me sane and amused every day: Dave Eklund, Craig Hisey, Andy Latack, Paul Levi, Craig Hisey, Brian Resutek, and Ryan Stayton.

I want to thank Mike Levine and to tell him I miss him a lot.

I can't thank my family enough for believing in me and nurturing my gift of writing. It is an honor to have the Adelson name. (Don't worry, Cousin Mike, I'm including you in this.) And I want to thank my second family, the Szulszteyns, who provided love and lots of good food.

And then there are my better angels, Andrea and Hope, who make every day feel like the best day of my life. I love you both more than I could ever put into words.

ABOUT THE AUTHOR

ERIC ADELSON first interviewed Michelle Wie when she was 10 years old for a story in *ESPN The Magazine.* A graduate of Harvard University and Columbia University's School of Journalism, he lives with his family in Orlando, Florida.

ABOUT THE TYPE

This book was set in Granjon, a modern recutting of a typeface produced under the direction of George W. Jones, who based Granjon's design on the letter forms of Claude Garamond (1480–1561). The name was given to the typeface as a tribute to the typographic designer Robert Granjon.